The Boundary Waters Canoe Area

The Boundary Waters Canoe Area

Wilderness Values and Motorized Recreation

JAMES N. GLADDEN

IOWA STATE UNIVERSITY PRESS / AMES

This material is based upon work supported by the National Science Foundation under Grant No. ISP-8204988. Any opinions, findings, and conclusions or recommendations expressed in this work are those of the author and do not necessarily reflect the views of the National Science Foundation.

James N. Gladden teaches in the Department of Political Science at the University of Alaska Fairbanks.

First edition, 1990

Library of Congress Cataloging-in-Publication Data

Gladden, James N., 1950–
      The boundary waters canoe area: wilderness values and motorized recreation /
James N. Gladden.
          p. cm.
      Includes bibliographical references.
      ISBN 0–8138–0151–6
      1. Boundary Waters Canoe Area (Minn.) 2. Wilderness areas – Law and legislation – Minnesota. 3. Wilderness areas – Law and legislation – United States.
4. Motor vehicles – Minnesota – Boundary Waters Canoe Area – Recreational use.
I. Title.
KF5646.B68G55   1990
346.7304'6782'09776 – dc20
[347.3064678209776]   89–26813

CONTENTS

Preparation of this book was assisted by a grant from the Ethics and Values in Science and Technology Program of the National Science Foundation, which is hereby acknowledged with appreciation.

FOREWORD

In the following chapters, James Gladden examines the principal currents of conflict over the status of the Boundary Waters Canoe Area Wilderness. This conflict was not over the traditional issues of mining, timbering, roads, or water power, but over the comparatively recent development of motorized recreation colliding with the equally recent advent of the wilderness movement and the growth of a nationwide preference for nonmechanized recreation in a natural environment.

The narrative shows how this initial dispute over wilderness status led to restrictions on the uses of motorboats and snowmobiles, thereby generating a chain reaction of political controversies. In the end, forces and preferences external to the Boundary Waters area appear to have prevailed. Yet, while the preferences of those residents opposed to the wilderness measures were largely defeated, it is not demonstrable that the well-being of the communities actually suffered from the restrictions intended to protect the wilderness character of the area. It seems safe to infer that the wilderness today attracts more visitors and money to the Boundary Waters communities than conventional motorized recreation would have done. There is abundant access for motorboats and snowmobiles on public lands throughout northern Minnesota, but the wilderness area is unique and the pressure of would-be visitors is enough to require entry permits. The principal threat to the motorless wilderness today may indeed be its popularity.

The economic life of the area has been impaired by decline of the American steel industry and resulting depression on the Iron Range. Establishment of the Boundary Waters Canoe Area Wilderness and of the Voyageurs National Park may in some measure offset the loss of income from the iron mines. The protected natural areas are continuing resources for the economic life of the region, which faces an almost inevitable decline in its traditional extractive industries in minerals and timber. Adaptation to changing circumstances is never easy for individuals or communities, and the burdens of change have not fallen equally upon all residents. Nevertheless, the adaptation of the region as a whole appears to be occurring.

The Multiple-Use Sustained Yield Act of 1960 (P.L. 86-517) represents an effort toward obtaining more diverse and efficient uses of the public land on a sustainable basis. A difficulty with the multiple-use concept is that many uses are incompatible if attempted in the same area. With the emergence of the environmental movement came an effort to preserve and protect some of the fast-disappearing areas of wilderness. But wilderness — where humans are visitors only and leave nature undisturbed — cannot coexist with mining, timber harvest logging, energy development, and mechanized mass recreation. Congress adopted the principle of multiple-use of the public lands, but provided no criteria adequate to mediate among conflicting claims. As a consequence, land-use priorities have usually been determined through trial by political combat. Exceptions to the multiple-use principle have been made through special single-purpose designations as national parks, wilderness areas, or military reservations. While priorities sometimes have been set for specific areas in dispute, political battles have been the customary mode of action in applying the multiple-use concept.

The Boundary Waters is a case-in-point in illustrating the difficulty of applying national land and water policies. Since the Louisiana Purchase, the Northwest Ordinance of 1787, and the Homestead Act, land-use planning in America has had a national constituency only when some perceived national interest has aroused a nationwide constituency. Local and personal preferences have governed most decisions concerning the uses of land and water. The environmental movement, the coming of popular ecology, and an upsurge of interest in outdoor recreation and the wilderness experience have created a national constituency whose assumptions, values, and objectives do not fit in with conventional assumptions regarding the rights of localities to determine their future. The environmental movement, drawing upon a nationwide constituency, has often prevailed in the United States Congress when it might have met defeat if the issue had been decided by local constituencies. The Boundary Waters conflict involved this division in values and in criteria for determining the public interest between local residents and outsiders, and the ethical differences involved could not be easily reconciled.

The Boundary Waters Canoe Area should be read against this broader context. It is not just a book about motorboats and snowmo-

biles versus canoes and snowshoes. It is a book about changing values
and conflicting priorities, and the difficulties of a democratic society
in dealing with them. Since the early 1980s, countercurrents to the
environmental movement have gained strength, but the public commitment to environmental and ecological values does not appear to
have weakened, and it remains to be seen whether environmental
values will ultimately prevail. The trend seems clearly in their direction.

LYNTON K. CALDWELL

Acknowledgments. Many people contributed to the preparation
of this book, although the interpretation of events and any mistaken
facts are mine alone. I especially wish to thank Lynton Caldwell,
director for the Program of Advanced Studies in Science, Technology,
and Public Policy at Indiana University, under whose direction the
project first took form. He conceived the idea, secured the funding,
and managed the project in the early stages. The National Science
Foundation's Ethics and Values in Science and Technology Program
(EVIST) provided the funding to carry out the research, including two
field trips to Minnesota in 1983. Rachelle Hollander of EVIST assisted the project at various points, and Robert Bartlett was quite
helpful in providing critical comments and useful advice on the manuscript. Richard Andrews, Robert Hattery, Marjorie Hershey, Kenneth
Sayre, Vivian Weil, and Daniel Willard also read and contributed
critical insights on the manuscript as it evolved.

Special thanks goes to Robert Hattery, whose company I enjoyed
greatly while on a two-week canoe trip through parts of the area in the
study. Several individuals in the U.S. Forest Service provided me with
essential research materials and useful insights. I particularly want to
thank Tovio Sober, along with Dorothy Anderson, Gary Lidholm,
David Lime, and Paul Smith, who also aided me during work on the
project. Miron Heinselman of the Friends of the Boundary Waters
Wilderness gladly shared ideas and information, as did other Friends
members. These include Charles Dayton, Janet Green, Harriet
Lykken, Brian O'Neill, Richard Rapson, and Melissa Watson. Sheila
Ballavance of the Boundary Waters Conservation Alliance patiently

answered many questions and provided valuable source materials. Other Alliance members who assisted me are Woods Davis, Bruce Kerfoot, Robert Olson, Russell Robertson, and Frank Salerno. Others who gave their time, opened their files, and in some cases commented on parts of the manuscript are Gary Ballman, Robert Cary, Harry Drabik, Gene Gaetke, Timothy Knopp, Lawrence Merriam, John Pegors, James Pete, Newell Searle, Jon Waters, and Julius Wolf.

I also wish to express gratitude to the staff members who assisted me during research at the Minneapolis Public Library, Minnesota Historical Society, and Northeast Minnesota Historical Center. Special thanks goes to Sandra Bruce, Christine Gilbert, Linda Ilgenfritz, and Robin Miessen for their unflagging support in manuscript preparation. Lastly, I wish to acknowledge Andrew Yurkovsky for his editorial work and to thank Bill Silag for moving the book along toward completion.

TO MY PARENTS

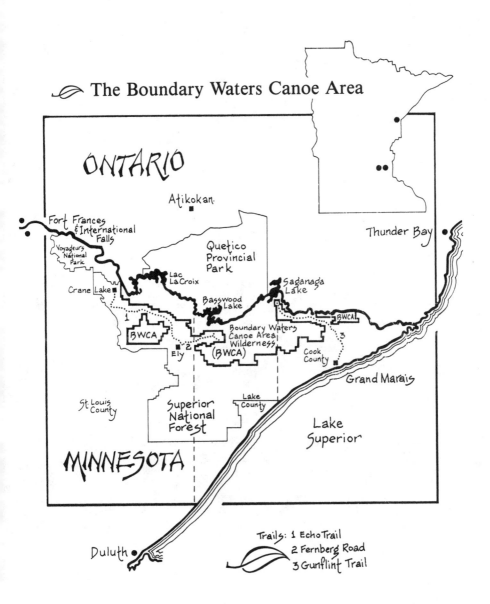

The Boundary Waters Canoe Area

ONTARIO

Atikokan

Fort Frances
& International
Falls

Voyageurs
National
Park

Thunder Bay

Quetico
Provincial
Park

Lac
LaCroix

Crane Lake

Saganaga
Lake

Basswood
Lake

1

BWCA

BWCA

2

Boundary Waters
Canoe Area
Wilderness
(BWCA)

Ely

3

Cook
County

St. Louis
County

Grand Marais

Superior
National
Forest

Lake
County

Lake
Superior

MINNESOTA

Duluth

Trails: 1 Echo Trail
2 Fernberg Road
3 Gunflint Trail

1 ✑ The Wilderness Concept

Introduction. There is a forested region in northeastern Minnesota broken by numerous lakes and streams. The short distance between the surface water areas makes the region ideal terrain for canoeists, who can portage from one lake to the next. This region, which has a reputation for its qualities as a canoe area and covers 1,075,000 acres, is managed by the U.S. Forest Service as part of the Superior National Forest. The scenic beauty of the Boundary Waters Canoe Area (BWCA) Wilderness draws visitors from across the nation, and the area sustains a heavy demand for outdoor recreation. A serenity pervades this wilderness area, but it has been in the center of several political battles over what public uses should be allowed.

The designation and management of wilderness areas often constitute a point of tension between local and national interests. The

U.S. Congress selects wilderness areas from public lands owned by the federal government. These areas, however, often lie close to communities where the interests of local populations are affected. The different views on how to manage these areas can generate intense political conflict. Residents often think that outside interests in pushing to establish wilderness areas disregard their concerns. The local population feels threatened by proposed changes in policies on the use of resources on public lands. People who live outside the region and advocate preserving such areas argue that retaining wild land is in the national interest.

This work analyzes the conflict between two types of recreation users: one group that uses motorized equipment for travel and one that does not. As a case study, the BWCA shows the interests, concerns, and anxieties of area residents over the wilderness issue. It also shows the values of political actors who seek to reserve some public lands in a natural condition for low-density, nonmotorized recreation. Congress included the BWCA as part of the original land endowment of the Wilderness Act of 1964, but the area was marked for future conflict from the start. The canoe area was granted use exceptions that did not apply to other wilderness units: section 4 (d)(5) permitted logging and motorized recreation. The area has had a long history of land use conflicts, dating from the early twentieth century. The most recent controversy, focusing on the use of motorized equipment for recreation, led to passage of the 1978 Boundary Waters Canoe Area Wilderness Act (P.L. 95-495).

Any study of what causes local turmoil over wilderness management issues must look at the different views of what forms of recreation are appropriate on public lands. In a pluralist, democratic society different forms should be and are allowed on federal lands. The critical question—what uses should be allowed on which particular areas—becomes contentious when an established form of recreation is displaced by the growth of a new user group. For example, light recreation use in the boundary waters area earlier in the twentieth century meant that visitors with motors seldom came into contact with canoeists, and so there was no conflict. But it is reasonable to conclude that even then some visitors who used canoes were philosophically opposed to the presence of motors in the lakes region. As recreation use by both groups increased, political conflict was inevitable.

The Boundary Waters became a political issue as a result of technical changes in the way people traveled across water, ice, and snow. Conflict between user groups also grew out of changes in social attitudes toward the natural world, as Americans generally became more aware of environmental quality issues. Those who wanted to eliminate motor use in the area held that contact with engines interfered with their wilderness experience. Most local people argued that using motors made travel easier and faster in the area, thereby enhancing the quality of their leisure time. These conflicting views on the role of motors in the area reflected a deep split in thought over how to define wilderness. And these different views on the meaning of wilderness raised the policy question of the appropriate recreational use of certain federally owned lands.

The BWCA case illustrates a classic confrontation between two sets of interests over how best to manage public lands for recreation. The dispute was over preferred methods of travel in the border lakes, not over problems of ecological damage. Unlike mining or logging, the limited use of motors did not significantly affect the canoe area's physical or biological elements. But such use did irritate visitors who preferred to travel without motors and those who objected to their presence on aesthetic grounds. The border lakes case in northeastern Minnesota was thus a political conflict between different user groups over whether motorized or nonmotorized forms of recreation should prevail. Many local people felt they were being forced by outsiders to make sacrifices so that others, most of whom lived outside their communities, could use the wilderness area in a way only they enjoyed. Canoeists with a purist vision of the border lakes region believed they were being deprived of their preferred form of recreation.

To get a better idea of the reasons for the bitter intensity of the dispute, this work examines the political events associated with conflicts over motor use in Minnesota's canoe area. As the political issue over motors grew, two coalitions of interest groups, the Friends of the Boundary Waters Wilderness and the Boundary Waters Conservation Alliance, organized to influence the policy process. Each coalition held its own views on what form of travel was appropriate in the border lakes region. The Friends sought to exclude motors, while the Alliance wished to retain the levels of motor use established by federal regulations in 1965. Their different policy positions emerged in the arguments advanced in partisan literature, newspaper editorials, congressional and administrative hearings, and other public opinion outlets.

A study of this conflict over motorized recreation on federal lands shows that public attitudes toward the designation and management of wilderness are complex. The actors on both sides of the issue took strong positions supporting or opposing the continued use of motors in the area. The conflict appeared to go deeper than individual preference for how to travel in the Boundary Waters. It raised the basic question of how human beings should relate as a society to the natural environment.

The Case Summarized. In 1975 James Oberstar, the U.S. representative from the Eighth District in northeastern Minnesota, introduced a bill for managing the canoe area. To resolve a growing conflict, Oberstar proposed dividing the area between wilderness use and multiple use, but the idea found little support in his district. Most residents accepted the recreation patterns that had been established in regulations issued by Secretary of Agriculture Freeman in 1965. The environmental community in Minnesota agreed that new legislation was needed to resolve conflicts but opposed removing some 400,000 acres of the area from wilderness designation. Responding to Oberstar's bill, environmental groups formed the Friends and worked to ban all motor use in the area. In 1976 Donald Fraser, the U.S. representative from the Fifth District in Minneapolis, submitted a wilderness bill to eliminate completely all uses but nonmotorized recreation. The Alliance was organized in Duluth a year later to protect established levels of motorized travel. As the policy process developed, both sides became hardened in their positions and compromise became impossible.

Each coalition attacked the motives and tactics of the other in an effort to win political support. The Friends viewed the Alliance as selfish because the Alliance opposed setting aside the entire one-million acre canoe area for forms of recreation that excluded motorized travel, such as canoeing and cross-country skiing. The antimotor forces pointed out that all other lakes on public lands in northern Minnesota were open for motor use. The Alliance likewise perceived the Friends as selfish because the Friends did not want to share the canoe area with those who chose to use motors for traveling in the wilderness. The Alliance claimed that the Friends distorted the environmental effects of motor travel to gain political support for its policy goals. It asserted that the Friends tried to impress upon the public that the canoe area would be destroyed unless motor use was banned. The Friends in turn charged that the Alliance distorted the real issues in order to enhance its public support. The goal of the Friends, as portrayed by the Alliance, was to urge the federal government to buy more land and tighten resource use rules to push private interests aside. The Friends cited an incident on Vermilion Lake involving a wilderness boundary issue as an effort by the Alliance to circulate false information about what sort of bill the Friends wanted to pass.

Some residents of northeastern Minnesota resorted to acts of civil disobedience to protest a snowmobile ban in the BWCA imposed by Secretary of Agriculture Butz in 1976. The secretary changed the regulations issued by Freeman in 1965 allowing snowmobile use, claiming that the Wilderness Act of 1964 gave him the authority to do so. After the BWCA Wilderness Act was passed, the Ely-Winton Alliance, newly incorporated from the former chapter of the old alliance, and the state of Minnesota initiated court action against the federal government. They argued that certain provisions of the BWCA Wilderness Act violated the U.S. Constitution. The U.S. District Court in Duluth upheld the law on all points, and its opinion was confirmed by the U.S. Court of Appeals for the Eighth Circuit in Saint Louis. The Alliance, however, remained dissatisfied with the new management rules for motor use.

Recreation Conflicts. In a democratic political system, federal agencies managing public lands are subjected to pressures from a variety of interests in the private sector. Questions of how to use natural areas are raised when citizens define a wilderness experience in different ways. Owing to a tradition of two forms of recreational travel, this problem has been accentuated in the Boundary Waters area. Some visitors use motorboats and snowmobiles, while others rely on unaided physical effort, traveling in canoes or on snowshoes and Nordic skis. Both forms of travel have undergone technical design improvements, including the use of lighter and stronger construction materials. The basic distinction between human muscle and the internal combustion engine as power sources, however, remains unchanged.

These travel methods became symbolic of divergent views of two types of visitors to the border lakes. Most people who used paddle canoes, for example, objected to encounters with outboard motors. The sight and sound of motors reminded them of the very thing they sought temporary escape from; it meant that they had not left behind the artifacts of modern industrialized society. Those who opposed motors asserted that encounters with mechanized equipment defeated the purpose for which they entered the border lakes. Such encounters lowered the quality of the wilderness experience they sought.

Those who wanted to continue using motors in the Boundary Waters saw travel as a matter of personal choice that the federal government did not have a right to regulate. They claimed that the use of motorboats in no way interfered with the quality of their outdoor experience. The pro-motor visitors argued that the irritation with motors expressed by paddle canoeists showed only that they were unwilling to share the area with others. Pointing to a tradition of motorized travel in the area, they asserted that it was sensible to use technical advances in water and snow travel. The pro-motor visitors also argued that fiberglass canoes and nylon tents were as much artifacts of modern technical society as were internal combustion engines.

These differences in outlook frustrated many canoeists, whose sense of wilderness was compromised by contact with motors. Those who saw the advantages of motorboats and snowmobiles for quick and easy travel were disappointed by restrictions imposed by the 1978 BWCA Wilderness Act. For many promotor people, canoes became a symbol for extremists in the environmentalist movement who used the political system to force their value choices on others. Neither side was fully satisfied with the outcome, although the antimotor forces got more of what they wanted.

Conflicting Values. The critical question throughout the political conflict was whether motors should be used for recreation in the border lakes wilderness. The issue was especially problematic because outboard motors had been used on boats since they first became available in the 1920s. People accustomed to motorized travel did not want to lose what they viewed as an established right, especially for what they regarded as less than sound reasons. Some motor users asserted that nonmotor users were trying to reserve the area for their exclusive use. This resentment was compounded in the case of snowmobile users, as the one million–acre canoe area received slight recreational use in the winter. Snowmobile users argued that encounters with visitors using Nordic skis or snowshoes were quite rare. Many residents viewed snowmobile use as an important form of recreation and a potential source of tourist revenue for area businesses.

Many pro-motor interests objected to reserving the entire area for a small number of visitors who sought a particular type of wilderness experience. Their pragmatic approach to the use of motors held that humans should apply new technologies and adapt nature to preferred uses. These same interests claimed that using or not using motors for travel was a matter of individual choice and not a concern of government. Some argued that because the canoe area was federal land all citizens should be able to travel in it as they chose. To them, excluding motors seemed elitist. Many of their arguments on the issue of motor use were decidedly against environmentalists and the federal government.

Most residents appeared to favor continuing motor use at levels established in 1965, while many visitors who came from outside northeastern Minnesota wanted to visit the area without encountering motors. Many residents in the region saw the issue as a struggle between local autonomy and interference by outsiders. Stricter rules governing motor travel seemed unfair; residents would have to bear the costs, while the benefits of such a policy decision would go to others. The political activists who opposed travel by motors claimed that motorized equipment did not belong in the BWCA. They argued that motors lowered the quality of their contact with the wilderness terrain. They supported this contention by noting that recreation opportunities were not fairly distributed. Motor use was allowed in many areas, but the BWCA was the only one in the nation where an extended canoe camping trip was possible. Also, the other two million acres of the Superior National Forest, which contained numerous lakes, were available for motorized recreation.

Technology and Wilderness. During its history, the United States has been guided by values promoting the economic development of natural resources. The idea has been to reshape the natural world for the material benefit of human beings. The application of this idea has converted much of the North American wilderness into an environment adapted to human ends. In the nineteenth century, American values concerning the environment were almost wholly utilitarian and based on the idea of economic benefits. Most people, through the perspective of their cultural values, viewed wilderness as wastelands. The only virtue of such wild areas lay in their economic potential to yield resource commodities. By 1935, however, preserving wilderness on federal lands had become a policy goal of a small group of people who formed the Wilderness Society. This interest group, as well as other advocates of preserving wild lands, viewed such areas as places where the public could enjoy a special type of contact with nature.

The preservation forces were highly gratified when Congress passed the Wilderness Act in 1964 (P.L. 88-577). Greater interest in outdoor recreation by the American public helped to spur passage of the bill. Also, the continued loss of wild lands to various forms of economic development convinced Congress that a statute was needed to protect some remaining areas. The Wilderness Act was an indication that public attitudes toward the environment were undergoing changes. A new way of looking at nature was emerging that put greater value on preserving some land in a condition unmodified by human actions.

The environmental movement helped to form new social attitudes that encouraged people to cooperate with and adapt to the natural world. The advanced technologies of modern civilization gave society the means to overrun all corners of the planet, but a new attitude toward the environment led to political efforts to preserve some natural areas from interference by humans. Trips into wilderness areas encouraged visitors to reflect on the meaning of things, free from the sights and sounds of the modern world. America's cultural values began to include the view that wild lands, as well as industrial parks, were needed to enjoy a higher quality of life. This new perspective required that humans apply modern technology to the natural environment in a selective manner. It meant rejecting certain types of equipment on some lands, such as motors in wilderness areas. Other artifacts, such as aluminum canoes and freeze-dried food, were acceptable because they made camping trips easier but did not alter the experience of direct contact with nature sought by the visitor.

The development of new technologies can generate social conflicts that did not exist before. This appears to be the situation in the policy dispute over recreation in the border lakes. When the first outboard motors were used in the area, only a few people entered the area for recreation and contact of any kind between visitors was rare. With an increased demand in outdoor recreation, the stage was set for political conflict. The motor use issue was intensified by technical improvements in recreation equipment. Outboard motors became more powerful and compact, while canoes became lighter in weight and more durable. A rise in prosperity after World War II put this equipment within the price range of many consumers.

The growth in recreational demand in the BWCA meant that, as more people visited the area, encounters between motor and nonmotor users increased. The expectation of an undisturbed contact with nature led many canoeists to complain about the use of motors on the lakes. With the noise and rapid motion of motorboats, it was hard for a canoeist to appreciate the natural beauty of the area. These visitors viewed the means of travel as an intrinsic part of the border lakes experience, not merely as a convenient way to get from one point to another. The dispute was especially hard to settle because, while canoeists were bothered by motor users, motor users were not bothered by canoeists.

As a federal wilderness area, the BWCA is unique in three respects. First, the ecology of the area has been clearly influenced by past human actions. The area's natural processes have been modified primarily by logging operations and fire suppression. Roads, cabins, and resorts have been built in parts of the canoe country. As a matter of Forest Service policy, these areas are now being reclaimed by the processes of nature. Second, the BWCA is much more closely tied to the communities near it than most other areas in the National Wilderness Preservation System. This history of human use has led some people to identify the Boundary Waters as a semiwilderness area. Third, the BWCA is the only large lake region in the nation available for extended canoe camping trips. The unique topography of the area makes it especially valuable for wilderness recreation users. The collision of these situations has created difficult resource management problems for federal officials.

2 ⁀ The Boundary Waters Canoe Area

Natural History. The BWCA Wilderness contains 1,075,000 acres and lies in the northern part of the Superior National Forest. This federal land is part of northeastern Minnesota, which is often referred to as the Arrowhead Region because of its geographical shape. The congressionally designated wilderness canoe area spans the northern parts of Cook, Lake, and Saint Louis counties. Its northern boundary lies next to Quetico Provincial Park, a 1,150,000-acre wilderness area in the Canadian province of Ontario. Five large lakes lie on the border between Canada and the United States, forming common waters between the two separately managed wilderness areas. The lakes drain to the west into Rainy Lake and then turn north and empty into Hudson Bay. The Pigeon River drains the eastern portion of the BWCA into Lake Superior, from which the waters flow into the Gulf of Saint Lawrence.

The Boundary Waters Wilderness lies at the southern edge of the

Canadian Shield, which is composed of Precambrian rock about three billion years old. The Duluth Complex, a geological formation with nickel and copper deposits, runs through the BWCA. The area's lakes were formed about ten thousand years ago, during Pleistocene times, by glaciation. The Wisconsin ice sheet gouged the lake basins down to bedrock, and they filled with water as the warming climate melted the ice.[1] Postglacial conditions have not favored soil genesis, and the soil that has formed is low in fertility. The larger, deeper lakes of the BWCA are lower in the nutrient content needed to support life. The lower, cold water levels retain high levels of dissolved oxygen. Lake trout, a prized sport fish, are found in the cold water layers; northern pike prefer shallow, grassy inlets.

The continental climate makes frigid winters and warm summers. The thin soils, broken frequently by the granite outcrop of the Canadian Shield, limit the plant life that can grow in the area. The BWCA contains a mixture of species found in the Great Lakes region, such as white and red pine. The boreal forests, to the north, contain fir, spruce, aspen, and birch. Among these forests are Voyageurs National Park to the west and Isle Royale National Park to the east of the canoe wilderness. Human intervention in ecological processes, through the suppressing of fire and cutting of timber, has altered natural flora patterns in parts of the area. Some forested areas in the wilderness boundaries are fire-dependent; aspen, birch, and pine need periodic burns to regenerate. Other areas, with species such as fir, spruce, and cedar, do not depend on wildfire for their life cycles.[2]

Animal communities in the canoe area are characterized by a food web that is still mostly intact, despite various human disruptions. At the top of the food web is the eastern timber wolf, a carnivore that preys on large herbivores such as moose and deer. The population density of the whitetailed deer, which are native to the BWCA, increased rapidly as logging operations cleared away the pine forests. The woodland caribou, however, which also are native to the region, had not been seen in northeastern Minnesota from about 1920 until recently. Logging operations sheared away the dense forests needed by the caribou for habitat, and heavy hunting helped to decimate their numbers. The population of the whitetailed deer increased as they moved into the cleared areas to browse. The deer were carriers of a parasitic roundworm, which didn't harm them but proved lethal to the caribou.[3] Open areas, which had been created by periodic wildfires, are needed in the forest to attract species the timber wolf preys upon. This need had been artificially met by logging operations brought to the region by European settlers. The Forest Service policy of letting wildfires burn themselves out will help to restore the browsing areas that existed before settlers arrived and began to alter the . habitat.[4]

Over two hundred species of birds and waterfowl inhabit the canoe country as either seasonal or permanent dwellers.[5] These include breeding summer residents such as the common loon and bald eagle. Some species of warblers raise young in the area or pass through on their way to nesting grounds farther north. Four major species of sport fish inhabit the area: lake trout, walleye, northern pike, and smallmouth bass. The first three are native to BWCA lakes, but the bass were introduced in 1941 to encourage sport fishing. Lake trout inhabit the larger and deeper lakes of the canoe area, while walleye and pike are scattered throughout the region.

Early Human Use. Use of the area by humans began about 9000 B.C., when bands of Paleolithic Indians moved into the region as the Wisconsin ice sheet began to melt. These people built a subsistence culture around the large caribou herds in the region, which was much cooler and wetter than it is today. By 5000 B.C. the glacial mass had melted enough to make the climate warmer and drier, bringing changes in the region's flora and fauna. The pattern of life centered on caribou hunting declined, and another culture evolved with the rise of the Archaic Indians, who migrated to the region and learned to make tools from copper.[6]

The Sioux, or Dakota, Indians occupied and used the border lakes region for several hundred years until about 1750, when Ojibwa Indians migrated from the east. The Ojibwa moved into the region because they had been displaced by Iroquois tribes and European settlers. The Sioux left the area and went west with little resistance, as changes had occurred in the ecosystem. In the Little Ice Age, from 1500 to 1850, the forests became wetter and colder.[7] As a result, there were fewer forest fires to produce browsing areas for large game animals, on which the Sioux depended as their major source of food. The Ojibwa, however, subsisted on a variety of plants, fish, and animals. They also were skilled in building and using canoes, which were ideally suited for traveling in this terrain.[8]

Several European explorers, including Duluth, Brulé, Radisson, and Groseilliers, entered what is now northern Minnesota during the seventeenth century. Sieur Duluth, the French explorer after whom

Duluth is named, crossed Lake Superior in 1679 and landed on the western shore.[9] Jacques de Noyon was the first white explorer to travel through the boundary waters area, spending the winter in 1688 at Rainy Lake. The border lakes became part of a route on which French-Canadian voyagers traveled during the fur trading era. These men, known for their endurance as canoeists, became part of the history of the region.[10]

The Seven Years' War in North America, fought by the French and their Indian allies against the American colonists and the British, ended with victory for the British. The Treaty of Paris, signed in 1763, transferred the Canadian portion of the French empire to Great Britain. When the thirteen American colonies became independent two decades later, there arose the need to establish a clear international boundary. The 1783 treaty, which ended the American Revolution, failed to do this, and the issue was finally resolved in the Webster-Ashburton Treaty of 1842.

The fur-trading era ended as a result of overtrapping and a decline in the market value of pelts. A gold rush occurred in 1865 around Vermilion Lake, close to the present wilderness boundaries. Some gold and silver were taken from the area, but the deposits were small. Logging operations began in the 1880s, and men harvested rich stands of white and red pine. Millions of board feet were cut and shipped, and by the 1920s most of the virgin pine forests had been cleared. Today northeastern Minnesota timber resources support a forest-products industry, which makes use of aspen, spruce, and jack pine for wood pulp.

The town of Ely was incorporated in 1887 and became a center for mining operations. The town is located on the Vermilion Range, whose iron ore deposits were exhausted through shaft mining. The rich hematite ore deposits on the Mesabi Range also were depleted by the end of World War II. As early as 1922 the Mesabi Iron Company began mining taconite, a low-grade iron ore, as the hematite deposits began to play out.[11] The Gunflint Iron Formation, which contains ore deposits that extend into the BWCA, has never been mined.

Public Land Policies. The Forest Reserves Act, passed by Congress in 1891, was used by public officials to set aside the first acreage that was to become the Superior National Forest. In 1902 Minnesota's forestry commissioner, Christopher Andrews, convinced the U.S.

General Land Office to set aside 500,000 acres of public lands as a forest reserve. They included forested areas that had never been logged but that had been burned by large wildfires in the second half of the twentieth century. The land was generally believed to lack any commercial value, but Andrews thought it would provide a good preserve for fish and wildlife. He secured an additional 141,000 acres of the future BWCA in 1905 and suggested to public officials in Ontario that they set aside forest lands across the border to remain in a natural state. In 1909 President Roosevelt established the Superior National Forest by proclamation. That same year, Ontario officials created the Quetico Forest Reserve, which it reclassified in 1913 as a provincial park.

In 1909 the Canadian and American governments signed the Root-Bryce Treaty.[12] This agreement established the International Joint Commission (IJC) to hold meetings and make recommendations on boundary issues of concern to both nations. The first major issue to confront the IJC in the 1920s was whether permits should be granted to E. W. Backus, an American paper mill industrialist, to build a network of dams in the vicinity of the canoe area. Backus, whose operations were in International Falls, wanted to use the water power and wood in the Quetico-Superior wilderness region for his paper mills. The dams would generate electricity for processing timber into paper products. Damming the water flow, however, would flood thousands of acres and destroy the terrain of the border lakes region.

During the IJC hearings, Backus dismissed the scenic value of the wilderness area along the international boundary as unimportant because few people visited it.[13] He argued that plans to develop natural resources and industrialize the region would realize a greater social good. The IJC hearings on the proposal by Backus began in 1925, and in 1934 the commission released a report advising the two governments against permitting the dam projects. The commercial empire that Backus had wanted to carve out of the border lakes region was never begun.

Ernest Oberholtzer, who fought strongly against Backus during the controversy, was a pioneer in the effort to retain wilderness lands in the Quetico-Superior region. Living in a cabin on Mallard Island in Rainy Lake, he looked at the boundary waters country from a perspective different from that of Backus. Where Backus saw resources for economic development, Oberholtzer saw in the same area a mosaic of often intangible but still important values to be preserved. In 1928 he helped found the Quetico-Superior Council, of which he be-

came the first president.[14] The council was organized to protect the
border lakes region from economic development and to establish it as
an international memorial park to honor soldiers killed in World War
I.

Oberholtzer and other council members attended IJC meetings
and played an important role in the 1934 recommendation to prohibit
dam building. The council's wilderness policy goals were buttressed
when President Roosevelt in 1934 signed an executive order creating
the Quetico-Superior Committee.[15] The committee's objectives were
the same as those of the council, but its formation brought official
recognition to the purpose of the preservationist group. The committee advised the president and relevant federal agencies on the management of the region.

In 1926 the secretary of agriculture, William Jardine, designated
three roadless areas in the Superior National Forest: the Superior,
Caribou, and Little Indian Sioux.[16] His action followed attempts by
local business interests to build roads in the canoe area for real estate
development. Jardine decided that the wilderness qualities of the canoe area were to be protected. In 1930 Congress passed the Shipstead-
Nolan Act, which prohibited the building of dams to change the water
levels of the canoe country.[17] To protect the area's scenic qualities for
recreationists, the act also banned logging within 400 feet of all shorelines.

In 1939 the federal government increased the size of the area and
renamed it the Superior Roadless Primitive Area. Its new boundaries
were similar in outline to the present BWCA Wilderness. In 1941 the
Forest Service divided the canoe area into two zones.[18] The Interior
Zone included about 600,000 acres that bordered Quetico Provincial
Park where no timber harvesting was allowed. The Portal Zone contained about 400,000 acres between the Interior Zone and the rest of
the Superior National Forest. In forest lands in this zone, logging was
permitted at the discretion of the federal managers. The Thye-Blatnik
Act was passed in 1948 to consolidate federal land holdings in the
canoe area.[19] The statute authorized the secretary of agriculture to
purchase or condemn and buy out private lands within the border
lakes area. Congress appropriated money to acquire inholdings in
1956 and again in 1961. In 1958 Forest Service officials changed the
region's name from the Superior Roadless Primitive Area to the
Boundary Waters Canoe Area.

Managing Wilderness. With passage of the Wilderness Act in 1964, the Forest Service was required to manage designated areas as wilderness lands. Most wilderness areas on national forest lands are in the western United States. The Boundary Waters Canoe Area is a noticeable exception; it lies in the eastern half of the nation, relatively close to large metropolitan areas. The border lakes area is the most heavily visited part of the National Wilderness Preservation System. It is also the only wilderness area that provides for extended canoe camping trips.

Because of the area's popularity, the Forest Service has been forced to develop a quota system to limit the number of visitors using the area. In 1976 the agency began issuing permits for different entry points into the canoe area on the basis of quotas, which limit the number of visitors in each of the area's travel zones.

The Forest Service limits the number of visitors in the canoe wilderness to protect its physical, biological, and psychological *carrying capacity.* Carrying capacity refers to the amount of human use a given area can absorb before too much change occurs. Roderick Nash defines physical carrying capacity as "the impact of visitors on the nonliving environment."[20] He refers to biological carrying capacity as "the ability of life forms and processes in the area to withstand alteration as the result of human presence." The psychological carrying capacity of a wilderness area is also defined as "the impact of people on people." For example, the physical carrying capacity of a wilderness can be measured by water quality and soil erosion or compaction.[21] Its biological capacity is compromised when fish and game populations decline or avoid certain areas as a result of excessive human pressure, or when vegetation is trampled and cut. The psychological carrying capacity of a wilderness area refers to the attitudes of visitors toward encounters with other users. For example, visitors' complaints about crowding indicate that an area's social capacity has been exceeded.

Rules for managing the canoe area have passed through several changes. Arthur Carhart played a crucial role in 1919, when he was employed by the Forest Service to survey the area for its recreation potential. Carhart spent the summer canoeing through the border lakes area of the Superior National Forest. In 1921 he submitted a report recommending that logging take place only where it did not spoil the area's scenic beauty for primitive recreation. Carhart suggested that timber cutting be prohibited near lakes, streams, and portages that visitors used.[22]

The Forest Service has been managing wilderness lands since

1924, when the secretary of agriculture established the Gila Wilderness Reserve in southwestern New Mexico. The second wilderness reserve was established in 1926 in the Superior National Forest and included what is now the interior part of the BWCA Wilderness. Support within the agency for setting aside wild areas in an undeveloped condition increased. An inventory of all roadless areas in the national forest system resulted in the Regulation L-20 in 1929. This administrative decision gave the Forest Service chief the authority to set aside primitive areas and required management plans for each area. But the regulation was not applied in a consistent manner, and it was not reliable in protecting wilderness areas from economic development.[23]

Robert Marshall, who was a strong advocate of wilderness values, also helped to shape federal land policy. He served as the chief of the Forest Service's division of recreation and lands. Marshall drafted new U Regulations, which replaced the ineffective Regulation L-20 in 1939. Regulation U-3 provided added protection for the roadless status of the three areas of the canoe country. These areas were to be managed to protect their primitive recreation values.[24]

The U Regulations provided greater protection for wilderness lands administered by the Forest Service. Some preservationists, however, were concerned about the agency's wide discretion to make decisions about managing wild lands. They feared that at some later time the Forest Service might reclassify primitive areas for logging, mining, developed recreation, or some other commercial use. Howard Zahniser, executive director of the Wilderness Society, asked the Legislative Reference Service to write a report on federally owned wilderness areas.[25] The report, issued in 1949, concluded that large areas of primitive lands were becoming scarce. It also found broad public support for preserving some remaining wilderness areas.

In 1956 U.S. Senator Hubert Humphrey of Minnesota introduced the first wilderness bill in Congress. This action prompted a series of bills that culminated in the passage of the Wilderness Act in 1964. The legislative history of this statute shows strong conflicts between those who promoted resource development on public lands and those who wished to set aside some natural areas. Some political bargains were required to pass a national wilderness bill and to set aside an initial 9.1 million acres of federal land. One such compromise was made on the Boundary Waters Canoe Area. Congress included it in the new wilderness system on the express condition that logging and established motorboat use be continued; this exception was specified in section 4 (d)(5).

The 1964 act defined wilderness as "an area where the earth and its community of life are untrammeled by man, where man himself is a visitor who does not remain."[26] More specific criteria for a wilderness included the naturalness, remoteness and size of an area, and features of "scientific, educational, scenic, or historical value." The statute also stated that there was to be "no use of motor vehicles" in wilderness areas unless specified in the law. The definition of wilderness as an untrammeled area and the basic criteria were rather general. The Forest Service, as well as other federal agencies, had to interpret wilderness in more concrete terms in order to administer such areas.

The Forest Service developed a purist interpretation of the wilderness concept, adopting high standards for deciding what national forest lands to recommend to Congress for wilderness designation. The agency preferred to manage areas in the preservation system with strict standards that banned all uses incompatible with wilderness values. These led the service to resist recommending any national forest lands in the eastern United States for wilderness status. Much of this land had been logged, farmed, mined, or otherwise modified by people, and it did not fit the agency's rigorous standards.

The refusal of the Forest Service to recommend eastern areas for wilderness designation led to passage of the Eastern Wilderness Act in 1975.[27] It established sixteen new wilderness areas and directed the agency to evaluate specific areas for consideration. In 1977 Rupert Cutler, the assistant secretary of agriculture, defended the use of less restrictive criteria for designating wilderness areas in the east. He argued that region's humid climate made it possible for ecosystems to repair themselves and return to a natural state, and the addition of eastern wilderness areas would help fill out the range of ecosystem and landform types found in the United States. Also, the eastern half of the nation held most of the population, which meant a higher level of demand for primitive recreation.[28]

Mining and Logging. In 1969 the Izaak Walton League filed suit against the Forest Service in federal court for the District of Minnesota to prevent George St. Clair from exploring for mineral deposits.[29] St. Clair claimed title to mineral rights in parts of the BWCA, and he had applied for permits from the agency to begin drilling. The League began court action before the Forest Service acted on his request for permits. The plaintiffs argued that the agency could not issue drilling permits because to do so would violate the Wilderness Act of 1964. They maintained that Congress had passed the statute to preserve the primitive qualities of the area, which they said would be destroyed by drilling.

In 1970 Philip Neville, the district judge, ruled for the plaintiffs, stating that preserving the canoe wilderness and mining were incompatible land uses.[30] The judge made the decision that Congress had avoided when it allowed some economic development in the Boundary Waters.[31] Neville's injunction, however, was dismissed by the U.S. Court of Appeals for the Eighth Circuit in 1974. The justices ruled that the legal status of mining permits could not be decided until the Forest Service decided to issue them to Saint Clair. The agency made no decision on the issuance of the permits, and this prevented further challenges in the courts.

Timber harvesting in the BWCA created another dispute over the use of resources. In 1972 the Minnesota Public Interest Research Group (MPIRG) filed a lawsuit in district court for the District of Minnesota seeking an injunction against logging in the canoe area.[32] MPIRG wanted to block the Forest Service from proceeding with timber sales for which it had already signed contracts with private companies. The group alleged that the agency had violated section 102 (2)(c) of the National Environmental Policy Act because it had not written an impact statement for the timber sales. The following year MPIRG and the Sierra Club's Minnesota chapter brought a second lawsuit against the Forest Service, arguing that logging in the BWCA was inconsistent with its wilderness status. Miles Lord, a district court judge for the District of Minnesota, ruled that an environmental impact statement was required. Lord stated that section 4 (d)(5) of the Wilderness Act of 1964, which allowed logging in the canoe area, did not apply when a conflict existed between protecting the area and cutting timber.[33]

The circuit court upheld the lower court decision that the BWCA timber sales were a federal action requiring an impact statement. The appeals court held, however, that the 1964 statute gave the Forest Service the authority to hold timber sales in the Portal Zone of the Boundary Waters. It rejected the arguments of the plaintiffs that the Wilderness Act banned the logging of virgin stands of timber in this zone.[34] This decision opened the way for timber cutting to begin. But U.S. Representative James Oberstar, who represented the Arrowhead Region, got logging companies to agree to a moratorium on cutting until the issue could be resolved by new legislation.[35]

Summary. As a natural area, the BWCA is vulnerable to human actions that change it in ways that allow humans to use it for different purposes. The early years of political conflict over how to use the Boundary Waters area revealed clear differences in attitudes toward nature. Some people wanted to build roads and summer cottages and construct dams and log trees. They viewed nature, and the canoe area in particular, from a utilitarian perspective. Others wanted to preserve the area as a region untouched by economic development.

The issue of motorized recreation, which arose later in the century, was especially problematic. Motorized recreation, within limits, did not disrupt ecological processes, but it did prevent many recreationists who were irritated by motors from enjoying the Boundary Waters. This did not become a matter of public policy until enough visitors began to argue that motorized travel was incompatible with wilderness values. By this point, however, motorboat use had become firmly established. Most local residents never gave a second thought to the idea that motors did not belong in the Boundary Waters. These two points of view surfaced in the political arena in 1956, during debate over whether to include the area in a national wilderness system.

The question of mining and logging in the border lakes illustrates the problems involved in managing wilderness areas. It took eight years of debate and compromise to get the Wilderness Act of 1964 passed. In some instances, legislators wrote ambiguous phrases or glaring exceptions into the bill.[36] In doing so, Congress compromised on thorny issues and set aside for the time political problems that at some point would have to be resolved. The conflicts over how to use the canoe area resisted a policy solution. The compromise in section 4 (d)(5) attempted to strike a balance between managing the area for primitive recreation and allowing motorboat travel and timber harvesting as established uses. Seen against the level of conflict generated over management issues since 1964, the compromise was a failure. Section 4 (d)(5) did not resolve the conflicting ideas of what uses were acceptable in the canoe area.

Management of the BWCA was so controversial that the only way Congress seemed able to deal with it was to avoid making a clear decision. The BWCA was designated a wilderness area, but at the same time legislators allowed uses that the Wilderness Act of 1964 declared were incompatible with such a designation. As conflict arose between interest groups over management of the area, the federal court system became a political arena in the struggle over mining, logging, and recreation issues.[37]

Political pressure increased until Congress again turned to the issue of what uses should be allowed in the area. Wilderness enthusiasts wanted Congress to ban logging, mining, and motorized travel as inconsistent uses. Multiple-use supporters argued that the BWCA was a semiwilderness area with a unique history of established uses. They maintained that timber cutting and motor travel were needed to continue the economic vitality of communities near the area. Each side drew clear lines of battle, and the struggle for new legislation was introduced in 1975.

It may be asked whether federal lands with a history of multiple use should be designated wilderness areas. In the BWCA case, action by Congress in 1964 created the conditions for a continuing conflict. Those who wanted the area designated as wilderness did not have the influence to do so unless they made concessions to multiple-use interests. The traditional uses of motorized travel and timber harvesting remained intact, although the Boundary Waters became a wilderness area in name. To make sense of this anomaly, it is necessary to look more closely at the history of motor use in the canoe country.

3 ✑ A Wilderness System Anomaly

Motors in the Canoe Area. The first efforts to open the border lakes region to motor use occurred in the 1920s. Local business interests wanted to build roads in the area and open its lakes to automobiles. They promoted the construction of summer homes, for which a market had developed during the increased prosperity after World War I. The Izaak Walton League, however, opposed a Forest Service plan to build roads in the canoe area, viewing it as a threat to the area's primitive qualities.[1] The League helped persuade the secretary of agriculture, William Jardine, to set aside three parts of the canoe country as roadless areas.

After World War II there was a dramatic rise in the use of airplanes equipped with floats for landing on water. The floatplanes were used to promote tourism inside the roadless areas. Land routes were not needed to gain access to private inholdings, as pilots could fly over the forest and land on lakes. Resort operators who owned inholdings flew clients into the heart of the canoe area. One owner, William Zupancich of Ely, built a lodge and several cabins at Curtain Falls. This was a scenic area where the waters of Crooked Lake thundered downstream toward Lac La Croix. Zupancich used the area to store boats and supplies for resort guests.[2] Those who wanted to preserve the wilderness character of the area objected to the resort business, which was made possible by use of the floatplanes. In the view of Oberholtzer and the Quetico-Superior Council, such operations were clearly incompatible with the primitive character of the canoe area. The sudden use of a new flight technology threatened the remote quality of the area.

A series of political maneuvers by preservationists led President Truman to sign an executive order that prohibited aircraft landings on water.[3] The order established an airspace ban 4,000 feet over the roadless area, below which no plane could descend. Truman's executive order was challenged in federal court, but his authority as president to create the ban was upheld on appeal.[4] The restriction on using floatplanes forced resort businesses inside the roadless areas to close. Zupancich finally sold his property at Curtain Falls after it had been condemned in 1963 by the federal government. The agency then dismantled and removed all traces of his resort.

The Forest Service used funds made available by Congress in the Thye-Blatnik Act of 1948 to buy out privately owned lodges and cabins in the roadless areas. Oberholtzer and his allies viewed the floatplane battle as a major victory in the fight to protect the canoe area from commercial intrusion. A new form of mechanized access into the wilderness region was halted. One conservationist predicted that the unchecked use of floatplanes would have diminished the wild qualities of the area and left behind a "minor and mediocre tourist trade."[5]

Outboard motors have been used to propel boats in the canoe country since they became generally available in the 1920s. But motorboat travel did not become a political issue until 1956, when U.S. Senator Hubert Humphrey introduced a bill in Congress to include the canoe area in a national wilderness preservation system. In defining proper uses for wilderness areas, the bill stated that motorized recreation was not acceptable. This provision, along with a ban on logging in all federal lands designated as wilderness, generated a wave of concern among residents of communities near the canoe area.

A Wilderness Bill. Senator Humphrey's introduction of the first national wilderness bill in June 1956 began another phase in political conflict over managing the border lakes area. Howard Zahniser, the executive director of the Wilderness Society, had drafted the bill that Humphrey sponsored. The senator included the canoe area in the Superior National Forest as part of the proposed national preservation system. The bill provided that all motorized travel would be banned in designated wilderness areas, including the canoe area.

Some people and groups in northeastern Minnesota actively opposed Humphrey's wilderness bill. They argued that the proposed legislation would create inequities among visitors. The American taxpayer would be "subsidizing and financing the summer pleasures of a mere handful of people who are able physically and financially to enjoy the pleasures of a true roadless wilderness."[6] Others opposed the bill because they did not want to see added government regulations for management of the canoe area. Some residents viewed the federal government as unresponsive to their interests and needs.[7]

Still others who opposed designation of the Boundary Waters as a wilderness area feared the possible economic effects. They argued that the proposed law might bring economic paralysis to area communities. Large parts of Cook, Lake, and Saint Louis counties included acreage in the canoe area. The county commission chairman of Lake County opposed the bill, claiming that it threatened the tourist and logging industries vital to the economic base of adjacent communities.[8] He did not want the border lakes to be reserved only for primitive recreation when its natural resources had the potential to generate wider economic benefits.

The town attorney for Ely argued that the proposed bill would encroach on the rights of the state of Minnesota and individual citizens. He claimed that Congress did not have the authority to enact such restrictive regulations on the use of resources. The attorney saw the bill as "an attempt by the federal government to establish a zoning ordinance in an area which it does not completely own."[9] Some of the inholdings in the Boundary Waters were owned by the state government and private individuals. He stressed that the bill "affects every person who owns an outboard motor, for the measure bans use of motor boats in addition to airplanes, automobiles or any form of mechanized transportation in the wilderness area."[10]

An editorial in an Ely newspaper argued that the proposal "curtails future development, restricts present operations, and in some instances cancels out entirely three of our major industries: mining, lumbering, and tourism."[11] Responding to the editorial, Senator Humphrey argued that its author was trying to "set up a scarecrow to frighten people."[12] The senator said that "violent propaganda outbursts will only indicate to the Interior Committee that complainers do not know what they are talking about." He argued that a close study of the bill would show that it would not harm the economic interests of Ely citizens but would establish a preservation system for the "permanent good of the whole people."[13]

Though a vocal group of residents in northeastern Minnesota opposed added resource use restrictions in the canoe area, others supported it. William Magie, who lived in Duluth and had supported policies to preserve the natural state of the canoe area for decades, argued that opponents of the bill wanted to exploit the resources in the area. Magie noted that in 1949 the Ely Chamber of Commerce had been a prime opponent of the airspace ban because it said a ban would be "the death of the tourist industry in Ely and northern Minnesota." He observed, however, that since the ban the chamber had advertised "the tourist trade has increased by leaps and bounds."[14]

Sigurd Olson, who lived near Ely and wrote books and articles that promoted wilderness values, supported Humphrey's bill. He argued that wilderness areas were places where visitors could experience "solitude, contemplation, respect and other aesthetic values."[15] Olson wanted the BWCA protected by statute to protect its wilderness qualities from the threat of development projects. He maintained that wilderness lands were becoming scarce and that policy decisions should be made to preserve them.

As the manager for the canoe area, the Forest Service opposed the bill. During U.S. Senate hearings in Washington, D.C., Forest Service Chief Richard McCardle had argued that the bill, if enacted, would "strike at the heart of the multiple-use policy of the national forest administration."[16] Testifying before the Senate Interior Committee in 1957, he argued that the Boundary Waters should continue to be managed as a semiwilderness area. Because the area had a history of incompatible uses and did not possess the qualities of a true wilderness, the chief argued, Congress should allow the secretary of agriculture to retain authority to determine the proper mix of multiple uses for the area. McCardle said that Humphrey's bill would hamper the agency's ability to administer national forest lands according to a multiple-use mandate.

The Saint Paul Meeting. In a meeting in Saint Paul in December 1957, Senator Humphrey responded to criticisms of the wilderness bill raised by residents of northeastern Minnesota. Humphrey, who arranged the meeting, wanted to consider their objections to the bill and make changes that would make it acceptable. Before the meeting, a group of citizens met in Ely to form a committee to represent their interests. Members of the committee wanted to see established uses, including motorized recreation, continued. The committee members agreed that "no change be made in lumbering as it is done now under the direction of the Forest Service; that mineral exploration and development must be allowed in roadless areas; and that outboard motors and motorboats be allowed to continue."[17]

The Saint Paul meeting was held in the office of George Selke, the commissioner of Minnesota's Department of Conservation. Humphrey arranged for the meeting to take place here because he believed the state government had a clear interest in how the canoe area was managed. Minnesota held title to 106,000 acres of land within the boundaries of the proposed one-million acre wilderness area. It also claimed jurisdiction over the 162,000 acres of water surface.[18]

At the December meeting, a citizens' committee from Ely asked Humphrey whether the bill insured the continued use of motorboats. The senator replied that "there was no intention in the bill to alter the motorboating situation at all, and . . . that the intention was to protect the rights of the motorboating."[19] He assured the people from Ely that existing rules for motorized travel were to remain in force. Humphrey read his revised language in the bill concerning the BWCA at the meeting: "Provided, that nothing in this act shall preclude the continuance within these roadless areas of any already established use of motorboats."[20] This exemption clause was included in all bills for preserving wild lands and became section 4 (d)(5) of the Wilderness Act of 1964. Committee members left the meeting satisfied that the exemption clause protected established levels of motorized travel. This understanding did much to quiet the fears of local people about the designation of the Boundary Waters as a federal wilderness area.

The Selke Committee. Growth in use of the Boundary Waters for recreation created the conditions needed to generate political conflict between motor and nonmotor users. This conflict in turn brought about increased management problems for the Forest Service. Among these were how to protect the area's primitive qualities and at the same time accommodate a larger number of visitors. Conflict continued to escalate between the two types of visitors. There was disagreement over the storage of boats along portages. Recreationists who used outboard motors carried them across portages and attached them to boats on the other side. The horsepower of motors and travel by snow machines also led to conflict.[21]

In April 1964 Senator Humphrey, Senator Eugene McCarthy, and U.S. Representative John Blatnik of Minnesota's Eighth District sent a letter to Orville Freeman, the secretary of agriculture. They were concerned about the struggle under way between the two factions over how to manage the canoe area. One group advocated the continuation of multiple use, while the other group wished to ban all but primitive recreation uses.

In their letters to the legislators, preservationists had charged that the Forest Service was allowing the wilderness qualities of the area to be destroyed. The legislators informed Secretary Freeman that they had received many letters accusing the agency of building roads and leasing timber, which the letters said diminished the value of the canoe area for recreation. These same letters accused the Forest Service of a "lack of concern and even complicity" in administering the area.[22] Humphrey, McCarthy, and Blatnik asked the secretary to put together a group of resource experts to "conduct an investigation, hold public hearings, and submit a report of their findings of fact together with recommendations for action on this situation." Believing that the issues would only become more confused with a "prejudicial airing," they urged Secretary Freeman to act quickly to avoid the harmful results of a "newspaper war" between the two sides.

Responding to this request, Secretary Freeman, in May 1964, established the Boundary Waters Canoe Area Review Committee to study issues relating to resource use. He asked the committee to produce a set of recommendations on how to manage the area. The secretary in particular wanted committee members to investigate alleged violations of logging in parts of the canoe area where logging was prohibited. The other issue the committee was asked to examine was the use of motors to transport people throughout the area.

Freeman appointed George Selke, the former commissioner of Minnesota's Department of Conservation, to chair the committee.

The secretary's appointment of five other members drew quick criticism from those who supported multiple uses in the border lakes area. The Timber Producers Association charged that Secretary Freeman had "stacked" the review group against multiple-use interests. The association suggested that several other people be added to the committee as a means of getting a broader range of views.[23]

In response, Selke said that "every member of the committee has had enough experience in his own field to consider the different points of view without bias."[24] He observed, however, that loggers and recreationists had different perspectives on how to manage the area: "Timber interests support multiple use of the area, a combination of timber cutting and recreation, and recreationists seek a true wilderness experience." A member of the Izaak Walton League from Grand Marais, who argued for protecting the BWCA from the effects of multiple-use, emphasized the nature of the conflict:

> There can be no compromise on degrees of wilderness or we shall continue to have a degeneration of the truly important values in the Boundary Waters Canoe Area. . . . Each group feels that the degree of wilderness should not interfere with its particular interest. It is evident that each group wants only certain degrees of wilderness. It is also evident that none of these groups has a clear conception of what wilderness really is.[25]

In responding to the letter from Humphrey, McCarthy, and Blatnik, Secretary Freeman noted the seriousness of the mismanagement charges against the Forest Service. He asked the inspector general of the Department of Agriculture to investigate the allegations. In August 1964 the inspector general submitted to the secretary an eighty-page document vindicating the Forest Service. The study found that "the allegations are without merit and not founded in fact" and that there were "vast differences of opinion" on how to manage the area.[26] The report noted, "Several witnesses stated they initially complained about Forest Service management activities only because they wanted the Department to review the present management policy for the area."[27]

The agency emerged from the investigation with an uncompromised record, but the charges cleared the way for thinking about a new plan for managing the canoe area. Secretary Freeman assigned this task to the Selke committee. The six members, working through the summer and into the fall of 1964, collected information and opinions on the issues. They read letters and reports, and in July held public hearings in Grand Marais, Ely, Orr, Duluth, and Saint Paul.[28]

Most people who testified at hearings in the northern towns opposed rules to further restrict timber harvesting and motorized recreation because both activities were important sources of income for local communities. They argued that current statutes and regulations, such as the Shipstead-Nolan Act of 1930 and the BWCA 1958 Plan of Management, were sufficient to protect the wilderness qualities of the area. But most of those who testified at the Saint Paul hearing wanted to sharply curtail or eliminate logging and travel by motorized vehicles. They argued that the canoe area should be set aside for primitive recreation use only. These people argued that establishing the BWCA as a total wilderness would be in the long-term interests of the region: it would perpetuate a form of recreation offered nowhere else in the United States.

The Selke committee completed its review and sent its findings to Secretary Freeman in December 1964. By a unanimous decision, the members recommended that preservation of the wilderness be the main goal in management of the border lakes. They suggested zoning the water areas for three types of travel—large motor, small motor, and nonmotor. Each member wished to preserve the values associated with wilderness, and zoning to control use of motors was a step in this direction. The committee also recommended that the secretary ban snowmobile use because it was incompatible with the area's wilderness qualities.

In January 1965 Freeman issued new directives for managing the area based on the recommendations of the Selke report. He increased the size of the zone where logging was prohibited from about 360,000 acres to over 600,000. He also limited motorboat use to nineteen routes covering 60 percent of the water surface and banned all use of snowmobiles. Aware of a potential conflict between the federal and state governments over zoning the waters for recreation use, Freeman stated that he would seek joint action with state officials "to put into effect a system of zoning for motor sizes, including a zone with no motors."[29] But he noted that restrictions on motor use were needed "to maintain the primitive character of the lakes and streams of the canoe area."

Many residents of northeastern Minnesota reacted swiftly to Freeman's announcement. They strongly objected to the reduction of multiple uses in the area. Some argued that the Selke report, which Freeman had used to make his policy decisions, was "in many cases an ideology unencumbered by facts."[30] They alleged that the report had not been based on an impartial analysis; its recommendations, rather, resulted from the predetermined values of the committee. Many residents also claimed that the report failed to take into account the economic interests and social values of people living in the Arrowhead Region. These people believed that their views had been ignored and that a decision was being imposed on them by a remote federal bureaucrat for the benefit of the canoeists, most of whom did not depend on using the area's resources for their income.[31] The president of the Minnesota Arrowhead Association opposed Freeman's policy because it "leans toward increased government regimentation and control and threatens the private enterprise system."[32]

The Boundary Waters Resources Committee. The Minnesota Arrowhead Association was formed by area businessmen to promote economic development in northeastern Minnesota. William Trygg, an Ely resident, formed the Boundary Waters Resources Committee in 1964 as a part of this regional association. As its first president, he set about collecting economic facts and transmitting local views on resource issues in the canoe area to the Selke committee. After Freeman issued the January 1965 management directive, the committee shifted its focus. Trygg and other members put together information to document the negative effects of Freeman's directives on local communities.

In a letter to Freeman, Trygg alleged that many parts of the Selke report had been based on inaccurate information.[33] He asked the secretary to delay implementation of directives until new studies had been completed. Trygg asserted that the 1958 Plan of Management for the canoe area adequately protected its resources. He argued that snowmobile travel allowed more people to enjoy the wilderness in winter, at a time when it received low use. Trygg also saw no need for the federal government to zone the Boundary Waters for motorboat travel. He held that the heavy timber in the area and the rugged terrain in effect decided where motorized equipment could be used.

In February 1965 Freeman rejected Trygg's request to delay implementing the new regulations. He did, however, agree to review any further studies sent to his office. Freeman asserted that the Selke committee's deliberations had been thorough and that all the issues had been fairly studied. The secretary stated that his decision was based on the view that the canoe area was a public resource of national importance that provided a unique opportunity for paddle canoeists who sought a special wilderness experience. Freeman argued that the new management rules would not depress the economies of the surrounding communities, as Trygg's study claimed, although they would require changes in the way residents used the area.

In March 1965 Trygg called into question the legality of the directive in a speech to the chamber of commerce in Hibbing, Minnesota.[34] The resources committee chairman contended that Freeman's directive "circumvents provisions of the Wilderness Act which clearly state that motors on boats and canoes shall be allowed where such use has already been established on principal waterway routes." He disagreed with the secretary's definition of established motorboat use and maintained that the nineteen routes cut back on existing use. In Trygg's view, this was a violation of section 4 (d)(5) in the 1964 Wilderness Act.

Based on the secretary's directives, Forest Service officials in Duluth issued a draft BWCA management plan in June 1965. In a reversal of policy, the proposed plan lifted the ban on snowmobiles. It redefined these vehicles in an artful way as "winterized watercraft" and allowed their use on the same routes that Freeman had established for motorboats.[35] This was the only change in Freeman's initial directive. Agency officials said the change clarified the original order. They asked all interested parties to respond to the draft management plan before the secretary approved the final regulations.

A report by the Boundary Waters Resources Committee, released in August 1965, claimed most residents of northeastern Minnesota believed that setting aside "vast acres of land as a primitive-type restricted area constitutes a waste of resources."[36] The report argued for permitting more motorized travel in the border lakes, as outboard motors gave visitors easier and faster access to scenic areas and fishing spots. Trygg's committee distributed a second report on BWCA issues in September 1965. It asked the secretary of agriculture to "comply with the intent of existing laws" and to continue established policies for managing the canoe country.[37] The report argued that because of its history of multiple use, the area was not a true wilderness. Phasing out motors, the report said, was a serious policy mistake, as it would reverse use trends and place economic strains on communities.

The groups supporting and opposing motor use in the BWCA continued to debate provisions in the draft plan for managing the Boundary Waters. The Izaak Walton League wanted to prohibit all motorized recreation, while Trygg's committee sought to retain established levels of use. Many residents attacked the motives as well as the policy goals of the wilderness supporters. A state senator from Duluth charged that small problems in managing the border lakes had been "blown up completely out of proportion to their importance, and circulated countrywide as typical examples of the desecration of this area by scheming, self-serving interests."[38] He said that citizens who lived outside the area were being "grossly misled by reams of false, contrived publicity disseminated by several powerful, righteous-sounding organizations." Such sharp attacks showed the extent to which a clear gap in attitudes toward use of the canoe area had formed between the two groups.

On 16 December 1965 Freeman announced the final set of rules for managing the area.[39] Freeman's directives established nineteen routes on which motorboats and snowmobiles could be operated and added two more snow machine routes to provide access into Ontario in winter. The secretary based this final policy on the unique character of the area: "Nowhere else within the fifty states do people have a similar opportunity for water-based outdoor recreation in a primitive setting on lakes and streams of unparalleled beauty."[40] He noted that the area was quite difficult to manage, as it did not clearly meet wilderness or nonwilderness criteria. This, Freeman said, placed the Boundary Waters in a special administrative position. Congress had made it part of the national preservation system but also permitted uses not otherwise allowed in wilderness areas. The secretary stated, "There is no pattern other than judgments carefully weighed to guide the management policy of the Boundary Waters Canoe Area."

The Snowmobile Ban. Communities in the canoe area adjusted to the new use patterns required by Freeman's directives, but tension between protecting the area as wilderness and permitting multiple uses created administrative problems for the Forest Service. This tension was exacerbated by the growth in public demand for recreation. More canoeists and motorboat users came into contact with each other, and this led to complaints by canoeists about noise and a diminished wilderness experience. Snowmobile use also increased between 1964 and 1974, and environmentalist groups objected to such use. The new BWCA management plan, written in 1974 by the agency to bring rules for resource use in line with altered demands, led to renewed conflict over travel by snowmobiles. Growing conflict over use of the area, including court action over mining and logging and increased demands for recreation in the area, had created the need for a new BWCA management plan. The 1974 plan continued to allow motorboats along travel routes established in Freeman's 1965 directives. But it proposed a ban on snowmobiles in the canoe area, except for three portages into Ontario, beginning in the spring of 1980.[41] Superior National Forest officials believed that use of snowmobiles in the BWCA was incompatible with its wilderness character.

To meet the requirements of the National Environmental Policy Act of 1969, the Forest Service wrote an environmental impact statement (EIS) evaluating the effects of the proposed management plan on the BWCA environment. In September 1974 Jay Cravens, the regional forester in Milwaukee, approved the BWCA plan that accompanied the final EIS. In October 1974, Charles Dayton, a Minneapolis attorney representing the Minnesota Federation of Ski Touring Clubs (Minntour), requested an administrative review of Cravens's approval. Among other agency policies, Dayton objected to revised regulations for motorboats and snowmobile travel. He argued that snowmobile travel was illegal in the BWCA according to the Wilderness Act of 1964.[42] That is, Dayton argued that banning snowmobiles in the area should be based on the 1964 statute, not the agency's discretion.

Responding to Dayton's objections, Cravens stated that the agency's prerogative to make decisions on recreation use in the BWCA was based on the 1964 Wilderness Act and Freeman's 1965 directives. Cravens contended that section 4 (d)(5) of the 1964 act gave the secretary of agriculture the authority to make regulations for the area. The regional forester cited the Freeman directives, which he said gave the chief of the Forest Service authority to determine on what routes motors could be used.[43]

In April 1975, Forest Service Chief William McGuire supported the decision in the 1974 BWCA management plan to terminate snowmobile use, with the exception of two portages into Canada. He decided, however, that the ban should become effective in the spring of 1975 rather than in 1980. Referring to the 1964 act, the chief stated, "As there are no specific provisions for continuing snowmobile use, and the Wilderness Act in general prohibits such use, I consider their restriction a necessary one to avoid conflicts with the primitive character of the area."[44] The president of the North Star Sierra Club was pleased that the decision "recognized the inconsistency between snowmobiling and the Forest Service duty to maintain the primitive character of the Area."[45]

Different legal interpretations of the Wilderness Act moved the conflict over snowmobiles into the judicial arena. Ironically, both multiple-use and total wilderness partisans opposed the ban, although for different reasons. The pro-motor interests did not support the 1964 act's interpretation that banned snowmobile use as a matter of law. Their legal strategy was to maintain that the secretary possessed the authority to decide whether snowmobile use could continue, although they contended that the ban was "arbitrary and capricious." The antimotor forces who opposed snowmobiles sought a ban on statutory grounds. They filed suit against the secretary for his position that the ban was a matter of bureaucratic discretion.

Protests against the Ban. The reaction of many northeastern Minnesota residents to Chief McGuire's announcement of the ban in April 1975 was similar to what had occurred when Freeman, the secretary of agriculture, had announced a ban on snowmobile travel in January 1965. The Boundary Waters Resources Committee, still in existence, organized a local protest against the decision to ban snowmobiles. The protest leaders chose two tactics to accomplish their goal. First, members set up four roadblocks on the main roads leading into Ely in May on the first weekend of the Minnesota fishing season. The roadblocks were established to demonstrate opposition to McGuire's decision and to collect signatures on mimeographed petitions protesting the ban on snowmobiles. Over 400 people helped set up the roadblocks and to collect signatures from the drivers of vehicles that were stopped. The protestors carried signs that denounced various environmental organizations that supported the ban.

Second, members picketed the Voyageurs Visitors Center, operated by the Forest Service and located just east of Ely. The picket extended to two Ely canoe outfitters who had expressed support for McGuire's decision to ban snowmobiles. Some protesters parked logging trucks in front of the outfitters' stores, and the owners claimed they were losing business because customers could not find places to park. This action ended when the outfitters requested a court hearing to secure a temporary injunction against the picketing. The Resources Committee agreed to end the boycott, and the court did not rule on the complaint.

The Saint Louis County Board of Commissioners went on record as opposing the snowmobile ban, and at a board meeting in Winton citizens discussed strategies to get Congress involved in the issue.

Some wanted to invite members of Congress to the area or to send lobbyists to Washington to explain their position.[46] Many residents thought that a new federal law to resolve management conflicts in the canoe country would be better than more decisions by federal administrators. The City Council of Grand Marais adopted a resolution requesting that the Forest Service reverse its decision and "develop a management plan that . . . would include the use of snowmobiles, as well as other motorized use equipment, on land and water within the wilderness area."[47] The city council argued that BWCA policies for summer and winter recreation should contribute to the tourist base of the local economy.

Some Grand Marais residents who opposed McGuire's snowmobile ban argued that their right to use the BWCA had been taken away. They feared that future decisions by the federal government might increase the size of the wilderness boundaries and place even tighter restrictions on use of the area. Others claimed that the ban violated a democratic principle because it prevented "the majority of persons from taking full advantage of the wilderness area."[48] Some citizens perceived a pattern of overmanagement, as uses that traditionally had been allowed in the canoe country were prohibited. They claimed that snowmobiles were already adequately regulated and saw the ban as a bureaucratic intrusion into local affairs. Many viewed it as an attempt by the federal government to favor one type of visitor over another; they felt that how a person spent his or her leisure time should be a matter of individual choice.

Conflict over a Bureaucratic Decision. Opponents of the snowmobile ban sent letters to McGuire protesting his decision, and action on the local level appeared to affect agency behavior in two respects. First, on November 1, 1975, McGuire announced that he would support the construction of alternative snowmobile trails in the Superior National Forest outside the wilderness boundaries.[49] Second, McGuire decided to delay enforcement of the snowmobile ban for one year to permit its opponents to exhaust all legal remedies against the administrative action. But he remained firm in his commitment to ban snowmobiles in the canoe wilderness. He justified the ban on the ground that snowmobile use was incompatible with the wilderness qualities of the area.

The environmentalists argued that snowmobiles should be banned because Congress had made their use illegal in the Wilderness

Act of 1964. In contrast, multiple-use groups maintained that the 1964 act gave the agency discretion over whether to allow snowmobile use in the BWCA. But, at the same time, these groups argued that the snowmobile ban was arbitrary and capricious in that the facts of the situation did not justify such an action. Loran Filter of the International Snowmobile Association argued that travel by snowmobiles in the area was legitimate because such use had been established before the 1964 act was passed.[50] Filter argued that the critical issue was whether the area should be used by recreationists during the winter months, and he saw no reason why it should not.

McGuire, however, viewed the dispute as "a conflict between types of recreation, not between commercial use and preservation."[51] He argued that the conflict was not based primarily on a concern for ecological damage caused by snowmobiles, nor on efforts by local interests to generate income from winter sports tourism. The critical issue, McGuire believed, was that visitors who preferred to travel without motors were irritated by encounters with motors, although the reverse was not the case. Filter and other snowmobile enthusiasts refused to acknowledge the conflict between motor users and nonmotor users as a real problem. They contended that the small number of visitors in the winter who traveled with Nordic skis or snowshoes seldom crossed paths with snowmobilers. If snowmobiles were banned, they argued, the canoe area would remain almost completely unused during the winter. The alternative policy would open the way to greater enjoyment by the public and additional tourist dollars.

Representative James Oberstar was pleased with the Forest Service's decision to delay enforcement of the snowmobile ban for one year. In October 1975 he had introduced a BWCA bill intended to resolve chronic and acute differences over management issues. Oberstar argued that McGuire's one-year extension was "a big victory for the people of northeastern Minnesota."[52] He contended that the extension would give conflicting interests time to work out a legislative settlement. Oberstar saw the extension as a means to reduce the political tension that had been created by the ban and hoped that it would promote negotiations leading to an equitable compromise.

The Duluth Snowmobile Hearings. In February 1976 Secretary of Agriculture Earl Butz announced that public hearings would be held on the BWCA snowmobile issue, and he encouraged all interested parties to participate.[53] At the April 1976 Duluth snowmobile hearings, Representative Oberstar proposed that the secretary of agriculture adopt the measures for snowmobile use proposed in his House bill. The bill contained provisions to establish a National Recreation Area (NRA) from the enlarged Portal Zone and to enlarge the Interior Zone and redesignate it as a wilderness area.[54] Mining, logging, and motorized recreation would be eliminated in the wilderness area. In the recreation area, logging and motorized travel would be permitted but mining would be banned. His proposal to divide the canoe area into a total wilderness area and a multiple-use area was not supported by environmentalists, who were unwilling to have part of the area declassified as wilderness. Among other things, some preservationists believed, this could establish a precedent for other wilderness areas in the national system.

Ronald Walls, an attorney from Ely, did not dispute the authority of the Forest Service to regulate or even to prohibit snowmobiles. He instead argued at the Duluth hearings that the agency should justify its ban, a policy that he called "arbitrary and capricious."[55]Walls objected to the format of the hearings, which did not require the Service to explain or justify its reasons for banning snowmobiles and did not allow for witness cross-examination. The Forest Service maintained, however, that the Duluth hearings were not an appropriate forum to debate whether snowmobiles were allowed by special statutory exemption; this was a matter for the courts, should the agency's interpretation of the 1964 Act be challenged.

A state representative from Cook, Minnesota, who testified at the hearings, alleged that the snowmobile ban was "strictly illegal under the 1964 Wilderness Act."[56] He contended that northeastern Minnesota residents were angry and frustrated because they were "faced with the potential of losing their recreational and economic opportunities in the BWCA." A Saint Louis County commissioner argued that the BWCA could be protected without adopting what he described as the recreational philosophy of a hermit. He claimed that "bans are illegal and discriminatory and wilderness serves a class in the minority." Another state representative from Eveleth, Minnesota stated, "There are selfish groups here who want to save the BWCA as a paradise for themselves—the wealthy."[57]

Others who testified at the Forest Service snowmobile hearings supported the BWCA snowmobile ban. The president of the Izaak Walton League asserted that "wilderness and motor vehicles are not compatible," and he argued that ample opportunities existed for snowmobile recreation outside the BWCA. A spokesman for the Duluth Audubon Society objected to noise levels caused by motorboats and snowmobiles, arguing that the aesthetic value of a wilderness experience was compromised by the sound of motors. Miron Heinselman, who the following year would chair the Friends' coalition to support the complete elimination of motor travel, testified for the Wilderness Society. He said that the BWCA was a national concern and that the majority of BWCA visitors came from outside the Arrowhead Region.[58] New management rules were needed, he said, to accommodate the growing preference for travel in the wilderness without motors.

The Snowmobile Issue Goes to Court. At the Duluth hearings the president of the Minnesota Association of Ski Touring Clubs (Minntour) had said that BWCA snowmobile travel was illegal according to the Wilderness Act of 1964. Just before the hearings the organization had brought a lawsuit in federal court against Butz, the secretary of agriculture. Minntour agreed with the secretary's policy to ban snowmobiles but disagreed that the secretary had the executive authority to make the decision. Minntour believed that the authority for the ban came from the statute. The ski touring association argued that snowmobile travel could take place in the BWCA in the future if administration officials changed the policy again.

In July 1976, while the lawsuit was pending, McGuire, the chief of the Forest Service, issued a decision on the Duluth snowmobile hearings.[59] For several reasons, McGuire decided to keep the snowmobile ban in place. First, the Forest Service had been unable to foresee the rapid increase in snowmobile use when agency guidelines to manage the canoe country had been written to implement the Wilderness Act of 1964 and Freeman's directives of 1965. The surge in snowmobile use now threatened to eclipse the wilderness character of the canoe area. Also, increased snowmobile travel in the BWCA was creating conflicts with cross-country skiers, whose use levels were increasing.

Executive Order 11644, signed by President Nixon in 1972, was another reason given by McGuire for banning snowmobiles. The order established policies for off-road vehicles (ORV) operated on federal lands and prohibited their use in designated wilderness areas unless "the respective agency head determines that off-road vehicle use in such locations will not adversely affect their natural, aesthetic, or scenic values."[60] McGuire asserted that the Forest Service possessed the authority to regulate snowmobiles and to ban them if necessary in order to protect the wilderness character of the BWCA. Lastly, he pointed out, snowmobiles had never been allowed in Canada's Quetico Provincial Park, the canoe area's sister park across the border, and it was the policy of the agency "to coordinate its management practices in the BWCA with those of Quetico so that the two are reasonably similar." McGuire stated, "The primitive character of the BWCA, particularly in the vicinity of lakes, streams, and portages where snowmobiles must operate, is certain to decline if snowmobile use increases."[61]

In September 1976 Secretary Butz affirmed McGuire's ban. Referring to the reasons cited by the Forest Service for the ban, Butz declared that fewer federal lands were available for nonmotorized than for motorized recreation. Noting a growth in public demand for winter recreation in wilderness areas, he argued that the BWCA should be set aside for visitors who preferred to travel without mechanized aid and without encounters with motors.

After Butz's decision, the Forest Service ban on snowmobiles went into effect in September 1976. The only exceptions to the ban were two routes leading into Canada through Saganaga Lake and Little Vermilion Lake. The Boundary Waters Resources Committee announced its intention to fight the ban, and Ronald Walls, as the group's counsel, intervened in the Minntour lawsuit challenging the authority of the secretary to ban snowmobiles. Other snowmobile supporters intervened in the federal court action. Some alleged that the ban was arbitrary, and others argued that the Wilderness Act of 1964 required "the secretary to permit the continued use of snowmobiling in the BWCA."[62]

On 18 January 1977, the federal district court upheld the ban, ruling that the secretary of agriculture possessed the discretionary authority to make the decision. District Court Judge Donald Alsop ruled that the Wilderness Act of 1964 recognized the special authority of the secretary in the case of the BWCA. This discretion allowed the secretary to ban snowmobiles if he chose to do so, although such a ban was not specifically required by law. In his ruling, Judge Alsop said the following:

> It was not the intent of the Executive Order to overrule the special provision. As recognized in *MPIRG v. Butz,* the BWCA has never been managed as a pure wilderness area, but rather is afforded a special niche in the wilderness system. The Wilderness Act did not change the BWCA management policy of multiple

uses, nor was Executive Order 11644 intended to change this management policy.[63]

To support his argument for the semiwilderness status of the area, Alsop cited testimony given by Richard McCardle, then chief of the Forest Service, during the 1957 Senate hearings on Humphrey's wilderness bill. McCardle had argued that the Forest Service should be given special authority to administer the canoe area as a semi-wilderness area because of its unique management history. Alsop noted that Congress had vested the secretary of agriculture with authority to manage the canoe area in order to maintain its primitive character.

Alsop stressed the problematic nature of the BWCA exclusion clause in Section 4 (d)(5) of the Wilderness Act of 1964: "It is unfortunate that the language of the Wilderness Act is such to foster continual litigation regarding the appropriate use of this natural resource."[64] As did district court judges Miles Lord and Philip Neville, Alsop declared that a firm decision by Congress was needed to resolve the controversy over what uses were appropriate in the canoe area. In an earlier dispute over management of the BWCA Neville had ruled that mining was incompatible with recreational uses. In another case involving logging in the BWCA's Portal Zone, Judge Lord stated, "If the Forest Service concludes that logging destroys the primitive character of the BWCA it must act to halt such logging."[65] Although these court decisions were overturned on appeal, the rulings against mining and logging revealed the confusion over what uses should be allowed in the one million acres of federal forests and lakes.

Summary. The history of mechanized travel in the BWCA included plans to build roads for access by automobile. It also included an intense battle over the use of floatplanes by resort owners to fly over the roadless area to serve their clients. The plans for building roads in the early 1920s were never realized, and an executive order in 1949 imposed an airspace ban. The use of motorboats began soon after the turn of the century and did not become an object of public policy until decades later. Travel by snowmobile increased quickly in the late 1950s and, along with motorboat travel, was attacked as inappropriate in the canoe area.

How a pluralist society allocates recreation benefits on public lands managed by the federal government is based on the idea of equity. There was a tradition of motorized recreation in the Boundary Waters in 1956, when Senator Humphrey proposed to Congress that it be designated a wilderness area. Humphrey's proposal galvanized many residents and especially resort owners whose businesses were located near Ely and Grand Marais. The banning of motors would have greatly disrupted the way that local people used the area for recreation and commerce. In effect, a quid pro quo was worked out at the Saint Paul meeting whereby Humphrey agreed to amend his wilderness bill to perpetuate established uses in the canoe area. It seemed rather odd to designate the region as a wilderness while not changing the uses for which it was managed. These uses included motor travel throughout the area and logging in the Portal Zone.

As will be seen, the residents of northeastern Minnesota argued that Congress had made a promise in 1964 when it permitted established uses to continue, and Freeman's directives of 1965 were written to carry out this legislative promise. In 1975, when U.S. Representative Oberstar introduced a bill to make major changes in managing the BWCA, many local people rejected it in favor of uses established in 1965. The antimotor forces prevailed but could not completely eliminate the use of motorboats and snowmobiles from the border lakes area.

Many local people, including Representative Oberstar, argued that in passing the BWCA Wilderness Act of 1978 (P.L. 95-495), Congress broke a promise it had made in 1964. That promise was to continue established uses, including mechanized travel. With the introduction of Oberstar's BWCA bill in 1975, Congress returned to the contentious issue it had failed to face squarely and resolve in the Wilderness Act of 1964. After considering several bills proposed by Oberstar, Fraser, and others, Congress passed the 1978 statute, which reduced motor use by nearly half its 1965 levels. To what extent does Congress have an obligation to honor its agreements? This difficult question in some sense assumes that democratic politics is static rather than active. In 1964 Congress was not the same body of elected officials that it was in 1978. The cultural norms of the nation had also undergone certain changes, with a greater emphasis on environmental quality values.

To say that Congress should not have the right to amend or even abolish prior decisions is to limit greatly the legislative process; the politics of public lands is a dynamic process that generates considerable debate. For example, federal lands in the National Wilderness Preservation System are not completely immune to changes in cultural values and political trends. By an act of Congress and the signature of the President the entire system, or parts of it, could be canceled and the lands opened for economic development. It is not necessarily true that once federal lands are designated wilderness the designation cannot be dropped and the management status altered. If America is forced at some point in the future to choose between a lower standard of living or a greater use of natural resources on federal lands, what its choice will be is unclear.

With respect to managing the canoe country, the Wilderness Act of 1964 failed to settle political conflict in the long term. Those who were interested in the future of the BWCA once again looked to Congress to establish a new management policy for the area. The mining, logging, and snowmobile cases revealed the problems of use conflicts in the BWCA. In separate decisions, three federal judges had stated the need for legislative action to clarify resource management in the canoe area. The lack of firmness by Congress about what uses were to be allowed led to public confusion and political discord.

In view of intense partisan conflict over BWCA management, the Congress appeared to avoid making hard decisions. It instead delegated authority to the secretary of agriculture to set policy for motorized travel consistent with established uses. At the same time it designated the canoe area a unit of the national wilderness system. This inconsistency between classifying and managing the area led to renewed political battles. Some interests supported a policy to make the canoe area a true wilderness with no incompatible uses. Other interests wanted to retain the area as a semiwilderness in which multiple uses were allowed. The political compromise in Section 4 (d)(5) of the Wilderness Act of 1964 ignited several policy issues that finally required Congress again to turn to the question of what uses were appropriate in the area.

4 ⤳ Congress and the Canoe Area

A Multiple-use Bill. The legislative history of the 1978 Wilderness Act (P.L. 95-495) was marked by intense conflict between two sets of interests. Both sides held different views about using motors for recreation in the wilderness area. Both interests generally agreed that limited use of motorboats and snowmobiles did not materially damage the border lakes environment. The conflict was instead one of recreational preferences, with the canoeists and skiers objecting to encounters with motorized equipment. The following two chapters describe the policy process that led to passage of P.L. 95-495.

In October 1975 James Oberstar, the U.S. representative from Minnesota's Eighth District who was elected to Congress in 1974 and replaced Representative James Blatnik, introduced a Boundary Waters bill. Oberstar's decision to offer a bill was prompted by the case of *MPIRG v. Butz,* a lawsuit over logging in the wilderness area, according to Charles Dayton, a Minneapolis attorney.[1] In August 1974 Dayton met with a group of environmentalists to plan legal action against the logging. In response to a proposed management plan, he sent an administrative appeal to the Forest Service opposing its decision to allow continued snowmobile use until 1980. The appeal led to the agency's decision to ban snowmobiles in the spring of 1975. The discontent in Ely over the decision provided the stimulus for Oberstar's bill.

Oberstar argued that the political tension over use of the border lakes region worked against the public interest, and he said that a legislative solution was needed. He claimed that the issue promoted a "growing divisiveness over its use and emerging resentment of people in the northern area of the state and nation."[2] The congressman identified three interests with a stake in policy decisions for managing the area. The first were preservationists, who sought the purest wilderness experience possible. They sought a natural area where all uses but primitive recreation were prohibited. Contact with motors reduced the quality of their outdoor experience. This group included paddle canoeists, Nordic skiers, and snowshoe users, most of whom lived outside northeastern Minnesota.

The second group was visitors to the Boundary Waters who used motors for summer and winter travel. This group included people who lived outside the region as well as area residents who used the wilderness during their leisure time. The third group of interests was resort owners and others in the recreation business. This group also comprised local business interests associated with tourism, such as owners of motels, cafes, sports stores, and gas stations. Their clients included visitors who used motors as well as those who did not.

As the federal land agency responsible for managing the area, the Forest Service also had an interest in proposed resource use changes. Its policies had been criticized over the years by motorized and non-motorized recreation interests. In 1964 Congress had required the agency to preserve wilderness values in administering the area. At the same time, the agency was required to allow motorized travel and logging. As a result of this inconsistent legislation, Forest Service officials found themselves caught between two sets of interests with different views on how the area should be managed. When Oberstar introduced his bill in 1975, the snowmobile issue was headed for litigation.

Oberstar sought to redefine the area's land-use status in a new policy framework that would end recurring conflicts. He proposed to divide the border lakes into two parts: a true wilderness area allowing only primitive recreation and a national recreation area in which multiple uses were permitted. The wilderness area was to be the old inner core, or Interior Zone, expanded from 618,000 to 626,000 acres. The former outer ring, or Portal Zone, was to be increased from 412,000 to 526,000 acres and redesignated as a national recreation area. The Forest Service was to continue managing the recreation area for timber cutting and motorized recreation. The redesignated wilderness area, however, would remain the exclusive reserve of visitors who sought primitive recreation. Oberstar argued that the bill represented a fair compromise between the parties involved, and he hoped that discussion would be stimulated to refine it into a workable solution.

Oberstar's Bill Opposed. Reaction from the environmental community in Minnesota was mixed. Charles Dayton commended Oberstar for "the extensive effort and thought he had devoted to seeking a political compromise on these issues."[3] But Dayton saw in the bill positive and negative things for environmentalists. The bill would protect a large area of virgin forest from logging and would prevent motorized use on canoe routes. He thought, however, that redesignating part of the border lakes area that had already been designated wilderness in 1964 "would allow snowmobiling in some areas of the BWCA and make it impossible for us to exclude motorboating and logging in those areas at a later date."

The president of the Izaak Walton League agreed that the bill would give away acreage that already had been legally classified as wilderness. Miron Heinselman, who in 1976 would become a leader in efforts to ban motorized recreation, logging, and mining in the canoe area, agreed that new legislation was needed to resolve the user conflicts. He saw Oberstar's bill as problematic, however, because "deleting some 400,000 acres from the wilderness system for a recreation area would be a bad precedent."[4] The environmentalists generally feared that the decision to reclassify nearly half of the canoe wilderness as a national recreation area might open the way to future losses in acreage in the national preservation system. Giving up federal acreage already classified by Congress as wilderness for multiple uses, such as motorized recreation and logging, did not appear to promote their cause. It might result in deleting parts of other areas from the system in order to make room for economic development of the resource base.

Oberstar introduced his bill again in 1976 in the second session of the Ninety-fourth Congress. Robert Herbst, the commissioner of Minnesota's Department of Natural Resources, responded to the resource-use changes proposed in Oberstar's BWCA bill. The state claimed the right to control use of the approximately 170,000 acres of water surface within the BWCA, as these waters had been defined by the courts as navigable. He pointedly rejected the "assertion of federal jurisdiction over waters in the area, as proposed in the bill." This rejection was based, Herbst claimed, on the idea that the bill prohibited motor use on water surface areas inside the redrawn wilderness boundaries. The commissioner proposed that the current management rules remain unchanged except for the extension of the Interior Zone to protect virgin timber stands. Herbst also objected to removing part of the BWCA from the "protection offered by the Wilderness Act and related federal and state laws, court decisions, and administrative action."[5]

Russell Robertson, an Ely resident and chairman of the Boundary Waters Resources Committee, was skeptical of both Oberstar's bill and Herbst's proposal. He argued that neither proposal contained provisions detailed enough to avoid future use conflicts.[6] Robertson objected to the state plan for increasing the Interior Zone and to its support of a wildfire policy that would allow fires caused by lightning to burn themselves out. He also opposed the state's position on mining in the canoe area. The state wished to prohibit all mining unless a national emergency arose. Robertson argued that it would be more sensible to make plans for extracting minerals rather than to wait "until there was an emergency and then let the mining companies tear up the land."

The resources committee chairman also argued against the state government's proposal to review snowmobile use in 1980 for possible damage to the environment. Robertson declared, "Snowmobiles have as much right as skiers or canoeists. We contend that the damage is being caused in the summer by canoeists, not in the winter."[7] Opposition to mining and logging died down as time passed, and workable compromises were built into the BWCA Wilderness Act of 1978. The conflict over motorized access to the area, however, intensified as the legislative process unfolded.

The Friends of the Boundary Waters Wilderness. Environmentalists in Minnesota began to conclude that they would need to organize a legislative effort of their own if they wished to ban all uses in the area except primitive recreation. Along with others committed to this policy goal, Miron Heinselman, who was a former research forester and ecologist employed by the Forest Service, made several telephone calls, which led to a meeting in May 1976. A group of citizens met in Hinckley, Minnesota, and formed the Friends of the Boundary Waters Wilderness.[8] The Friends was organized as a coalition to coordinate efforts between interest groups, and Heinselman was chosen to serve as its chairman. Decisions were made through an executive committee, which was composed of people representing the environmental groups who wished to be involved in the legislative effort. About thirty persons attended the executive meetings, and the consensus on decisions was usually clear enough so that votes did not have to be counted. The founders organized the Friends coalition to lobby Congress, and one way to accomplish this goal was to build public support for complete wilderness protection.

Leaders of the Friends agreed that the major problem with Oberstar's bill was his proposal to remove some 400,000 acres already designated as wilderness from the canoe area. The Friends approached Donald Fraser, the U.S. representative from the Fifth District in Minneapolis, and asked him to sponsor a bill providing total protection for the wilderness in the area. He agreed to do so, and in June 1976 he introduced a bill written by the Friends as an alternative to Oberstar's. The bill banned all logging and mining and would eliminate all motorized recreation.

In August 1976 the Friends distributed a booklet explaining its positions on resource-use issues in the BWCA to the public.[9] It noted that the adjoining one-million acre Quetico Provincial Park in Canada was managed strictly to preserve wilderness values. The Friends' booklet pointed out that over 70 percent of the visitors to the canoe area wilderness now traveled by nonmotorized means, while the number of persons using motorized transportation was declining. It cited a study completed by a Forest Service social scientist that found that "93 percent of the paddlers were irritated by encounters with motors."[10] The booklet argued that motorboats should be excluded from the area, as most visitors objected to their presence. It also argued that snowmobile use was illegal because this type of travel did not conform with the intent of the Wilderness Act of 1964.

In January 1977 Fraser again introduced his Boundary Waters wilderness bill in the first session of the Ninety-fifth Congress.

H.R. 2820 provided for complete protection of the Boundary Waters, banning all uses considered by environmentalists to be incompatible with wilderness. On the floor of the House of Representatives, Fraser blamed the current impasse over how to use the area on section 4 (d)(5) of the Wilderness Act of 1964, which he termed a "frustratingly ambiguous paragraph."[11] He agreed with his Eighth District colleague, James Oberstar, that a new policy was needed to calm the intense political debate that the issue had generated.

Fraser stated that the intent of H.R. 2820 was simple: to make the BWCA a true wilderness that allowed only primitive recreation.[12] His bill served as a starting point for discussion with pro-motor interests that held a different vision of how to use the area. The Friends pursued a vigorous campaign to recruit members for their cause. They mailed literature to interested individuals, many of whose names came from a list of BWCA visitors who had traveled in the area by canoe.[13] The financial resources needed to lobby Congress were provided by members of the coalition, and volunteers spent many hours promoting the coalition's goals. By the spring of 1977 the Friends' campaign had developed momentum.

The Boundary Waters Conservation Alliance. Many residents of northeastern Minnesota were opposed to any changes in statutes governing the canoe area. Communities such as Ely, Grand Marais, and Crane Lake had adjusted to the rules on motor use imposed by Freeman's directives of 1965. Patterns of recreational and commercial use had been built around these routes. Resort owners and outfitters had invested capital to market outdoor recreation services to visitors to the area. Many businesses had clients who returned each year to use the same motor routes for fishing trips. Some local observers, however, began to assess the growing strength of the environmental coalition. They were sensitive to new political currents and concluded that organized action was needed to fend off efforts by the Friends to change the BWCA management rules. If multiple users ignored the Friends, they might be displaced from the border lakes wilderness.

Oberstar continued to promote his bill as the most equitable means to resolve the conflict over management of the canoe area. He believed that his bill reflected a true compromise that both sides should be able to accept. During a speech given in October 1977 to the Minnesota Arrowhead Association in Duluth, the congressman restated the central idea of his bill:

> A law is needed that will spell out the rights, uses, and future management of that area. We've tried to shape a management plan in the interest of the majority of people living in that area but also in the legitimate interest of people who love the wilderness.[14]

Oberstar argued that dividing the canoe area into two parts and clearly defining the uses appropriate for each would resolve the dispute. Each side would then be secure in having part of the canoe area for its preferred use.

The growing support for Fraser's bill finally generated enough concern for multiple-use interests in northeastern Minnesota that they began to organize. In May 1977 a group of citizens from the region met in Duluth and formed the Boundary Waters Conservation Alliance.[15] The purpose of the coalition was to publicize the multiple-use cause and to lobby Congress for a bill favorable to the interests of its members. The Alliance supported Oberstar's bill but suggested several changes in the way it was written. This was accomplished by the coalition's legislative committee, which held meetings in towns in the Arrowhead Region to seek public comments. The committee then met with Oberstar, and many of its suggestions were structured into a new bill.

Robert Buckler, a former member of Oberstar's staff, became the first executive director of the Alliance. He stated that the Alliance was "independent of timber interests and Oberstar's staff itself." The goal of the new coalition, according to Buckler, was to "tell the story from the northeast Minnesota perspective."[16] The Alliance had an executive board and committees for raising funds, lobbying Congress, and building media support for its goals. The group's financial resources came primarily from members' dues and contributions.[17] As with the Friends, most of its work was accomplished by volunteers. Alliance members included area property owners, resort owners, outfitters, motorized recreation users, and others who saw Fraser's wilderness bill as a threat.

Growth in Conflict. Some residents near the canoe area remained opposed to both bills before Congress. Joe Skala, a resort owner who lived in Winton, a town just east of Ely on the Fernberg Road, expressed a view that summarized the fears of many residents. He argued that "both bills are potentially economically disastrous for the area."[18] Skala claimed that the bills were not specific enough, so it was hard to gauge how they would affect communities located near the canoe area. He asserted that the imprecise provisions could lead to varying interpretations, thus renewing management conflicts. Skala criticized Oberstar's concept of a national recreation area, saying it "failed to spell out the specifics, preferring to leave much of the management to the Forest Service." The resort owner objected to this, asserting that the agency was "tuned in too closely to a minority of environmentalists."

Jim Cherry, director of a Christian youth center on Seagull Lake, supported Fraser's bill. But he was concerned about the effects of a complete motor ban on area business interests. Cherry argued that the federal government was "morally obligated" to compensate operators who were harmed by the new land-use rules.[19] He referred to Oberstar's bill as an "administrative nightmare" because it was too loosely written to provide any clear management direction. Cherry wanted motor bans as a means to provide canoeists with their chosen form of recreation. But he also supported the continued use of small motors on some lakes to allow some tourist firms "to service the public, retain reasonably easy access to summer homes, and let old disabled persons see part of the wilderness."

Cherry's point about the obligation of the federal government to compensate business interests harmed by changes in management rules had some merit. Many firms located on the edge of the wilderness had built up a type of client who preferred to travel with motors in the canoe area. These visitors provided a significant volume of business for the resort owners and operators located on the edge of the wilderness area who provided outfitters services. Secretary Freeman's 1965 regulations had limited motor use to nineteen water routes, and many businesses had adapted their operations to these routes. The proposed ban on motor use meant the disruption of this pattern, and many operators were apprehensive about its effect on their business.

Although most people in northeastern Minnesota appeared to support the established use of motorized recreation, many residents of the southern, more urbanized parts of the state had different views. An editorial in a Saint Paul newspaper argued that Fraser's bill was "an attempt, quite practical from a scientific standpoint, to set aside, for this and generations succeeding, something of our heritage not dedicated to private aggrandizement."[20] The editorial claimed that the canoe area should be preserved in a pristine state for future generations to enjoy. It criticized the commercial motives of loggers, outfitters, and resort owners, arguing that they wanted to exploit the wilderness.

The claim that selfish interests were making private profit from exploiting the border lakes was countered by equally harsh charges from multiple-use supporters. An Ely newspaper derisively referred to Fraser as the "messiah" of future generations.[21] It also attacked environmentalists for taking what it called a dogmatic approach to wilderness purity. The editorial claimed that these people were "crusading for their pristine wilderness at the expense of violating the individual rights of a small minority." Although local people were few in number, the newspaper asserted, preservationists had no right to destroy the economic basis of their communities or deny them their chosen form of recreation. It charged that the federal government was being manipulated by a wilderness cult and called the Forest Service an "army of green shirts who have been drafted as policemen to guard their sacred place."[22]

Subcommittee Field Hearings. In July 1977 the House Subcommittee on National Parks and Insular Affairs held field hearings on the BWCA bills. Representative Phillip Burton from California, who chaired the subcommittee, appointed Bruce Vento to conduct the hearings. Vento, a congressman from Saint Paul, was the only member of the subcommittee who went to Minnesota for the hearings. On 7 July he heard testimony at the state capitol in Saint Paul. During this hearing, which was without incident, testimony mostly favored the Fraser bill.

The next day, Vento traveled to Ely and held a second hearing. An Ely newspaper noted that there was a mood of "resigned futility" in the town before the meeting.[23] Many people thought that the subcommittee had already reached a decision in favor of the legislation sponsored by Fraser. And, with only one subcommittee member attending, some residents felt that Congress had little interest in learning the local views on the management issues. The newspaper stated, "The wrong people are being blamed and the Fraser bill would reward

the people causing the problem."[24] It argued that canoe parties damaged campsites, as motorboat users seldom camped in the wilderness
area overnight.

Some supporters of multiple use claimed that environmentalists
were using blatant propaganda to misinform the larger public about
the facts on motorized recreation. Alliance leaders argued that the
Friends' literature portrayed motorized recreation as an immediate
threat to the survival of the wilderness area. They asserted that Fraser
and his supporters had no true interest in studying the full effects of
their proposed changes in resource policy. The *Ely Echo* criticized
Fraser for his statement that more studies of the Boundary Waters
problem would add little new knowledge to help resolve the conflict.
Fraser had argued that the controversy did "not derive from a lack of
information, but from basic philosophical differences about how the
area should best be managed."[25] Many multiple-use supporters also
objected to being written off as "antiwilderness" persons. They did
not think that logging and motor use diminished or altered the natural
qualities of the area. This higher toleration for multiple-resource uses
in the canoe area showed a clear difference in views on the meaning of
wilderness.[26]

About one thousand persons, mostly residents, crowded into
Ely's junior high school auditorium to attend the subcommittee
hearing chaired by Vento. Although not members of the subcommittee, Oberstar and Fraser sat with Vento and listened to eight hours of
testimony. Some multiple-use advocates parked huge logging trucks
and trailers loaded with snowmobiles and motorboats directly outside
the center. In a display of strong feelings, others who came to the
hearing hung Miron Heinselman and the Sierra Club in effigy from
the boom of a logging truck. Strong emotions were evident as the
chairman began the hearing to take testimony on how to manage the
one million acres that began just outside Ely.

The testimony was split sharply between those who wanted to
ban all multiple uses and others who wished to continue existing logging and motorized access. Some residents who wished to retain a
multiple-use policy were not enthusiastic about Oberstar's bill, but
those who attended the meeting appeared united in their opposition to
Fraser's bill. A Minnesota state senator called preservationists selfish
people who refused to make any compromise. He noted that residents
had already compromised in 1964 by allowing the canoe area to be
designated a wilderness. An Ely businessman argued against both bills
because he was "tired of the federal bureaucracy eroding the rights of
individuals."[27] He was concerned about increased land control by the

federal government in northeastern Minnesota. Several outfitters and resort owners spoke against Fraser's bill, claiming that it would result in their economic ruin. One resort owner opposed any new legislation that would force people living in the area to make further concessions to outsiders.

Sigurd Olson, a resident of Ely and a renowned nature writer, testified against Oberstar's bill. He argued that it would divide the canoe area in half, and "once fragmented there is no hope for a complete wilderness."[28] A resident of the town of Virginia who supported Fraser's bill objected to the curious attitude of some residents. She argued that they behaved as if they held title to the land in the Boundary Waters and that the government had a duty to manage the area for their exclusive benefit. She pointed out that the area was federally owned land to be administered according to national goals. Jack Ford, the son of former President Ford, also testified in support of the Fraser bill. He said that people across the nation were interested in the management of the canoe area and that it was not just a local or regional issue. Ford said that it was time for Congress to prohibit all uses that conflicted with the wilderness values of naturalness and solitude.

The Ely hearing showed the extent to which interest group positions on how to use the Boundary Waters had become polarized. It revealed a deep division in the attitudes of the members of the Friends and the Alliance. Vento's subcommittee hearing brought these conflicting values clearly into the open for the first time. Activists on both sides of the controversy began to realize that reaching their goals would take much time and effort. No middle ground appeared to exist on which the leaders of the two factions could meet and discuss their views.

After the field hearing David Zentner, the president of the Izaak Walton League, and Robert Cary, the newspaper editor for the *Ely Echo,* had a conversation. Zentner objected to the audience's heckling of Sigurd Olson when he testified in support of Fraser's bill. He called Ely residents rude and described their behavior as "ugly to the point of irresponsibility."[29] Cary, a multiple-use supporter, explained the outburst against Olson as a reaction to what local people viewed as hypocritical behavior. In earlier years, Olson had used motorboats and floatplanes as standard equipment for his outfitting business. Yet Olson had failed to acknowledge that he used motors for commercial profit. Cary asserted, "When these issues get involved in some sort of an issue of morality, some people feel the preacher could be expected to preface his remarks with a confession of his own sins."[30]

Cary also criticized the 1965 canoe trip of Lynda Johnson, the daughter of President Johnson, comparing it to Jack Ford's recent visit. He argued that both trips had been staged for the media to sell the public on a romantic but false ideal of wilderness. Cary noted that Johnson had been persuaded against her wishes to take the paddle canoe trip for publicity reasons. She had insisted that fresh water be flown into her, refusing to drink the lake water. She also wanted cleared campsites doused with insecticide. The national press, however, had reported the trip as though it were a rugged adventure in which she was in direct contact with nature. In a similar vein, Ford had testified at the subcommittee's Ely field hearing in support of a bill to preserve the wilderness. But his party had used floatplanes and motorboats to travel through some of the very same areas where the bill proposed to ban motors. This contradiction between professed values and actual behavior offended many local residents. Cary argued that such contrived media events helped the wilderness cause by projecting an attractive but false image to the American public.

One impression that emerged from the Ely hearing was the lack of unity among multiple-use interests, especially when compared with those who supported the pure wilderness ideal. The multiple-use supporters were divided over whether to support Oberstar's bill or to continue fighting to retain established uses. In addition, many local people failed to think through the larger political issue beyond the geography of the Arrowhead Region. The values they wished to see promoted in managing the canoe area were not shared with the same intensity in the southern half of the state. In August 1977 a Minneapolis newspaper published the results of a statewide poll on what uses should be allowed in the federally owned canoe area. The poll found that 49 percent of the respondents favored complete wilderness protection for the area, while 46 percent supported logging and motors in the area.[31]

The Washington Subcommittee Hearings. On 4 August 1977 Burton's subcommittee met to discuss developments on the BWCA issue, and Vento summarized his views on the Saint Paul and Ely field hearings. Fraser explained some changes in his bill to the subcommittee, noting that revisions in H.R. 2820 were meant to promote a compromise with multiple use interests. Fraser wanted to phase out motor use on certain lakes, as this would lessen economic problems for some outfitters and resorters. He also suggested that a few lakes in the wilderness area remain permanently open for motor use. He wanted Congress to authorize funds for buying out resort owners on specified lakes whose business would decline when motors were banned. He also proposed that funds be authorized for developed recreation, such as snowmobile trails, in the other two million acres of the Superior National Forest outside the canoe wilderness.[32]

On 5 August Oberstar introduced his third BWCA bill, H.R. 8722, on the House floor. He explained to his colleagues his belief that the dispute was not "between narrow local concerns and the broad national interest in the preservation of wilderness."[33] The congressman argued that this simplified view failed to capture the fact that local people, as well as those who sought to ban motors, had valid interests to defend. The new bill included several changes suggested by leaders in the Alliance, but the basic concept of dividing the BWCA between a wilderness area and a national recreation area remained. Oberstar wanted to set a clear resource-use policy in a statute that could not be interpreted against local interests by federal bureaucrats who managed the area.

On 12 and 13 September the Subcommittee on National Parks and Insular Affairs held hearings in Washington, D.C. Burton, who was widely known as a supporter of environmental causes, chaired the hearings. The mayor of Grand Marais was among those who testified in support of Oberstar's revised BWCA bill. He argued that supporters of the Fraser bill seemed to think that "the national benefit is so great that it is worth the cost of economic hardships and a reduction in the quality of life for the people of Grand Marais and all of northeastern Minnesota."[34] The mayor noted that preservationists could dismiss the negative effects on area communities of a policy to exclude motorized travel and logging, as they would not have to bear any of the costs. The mayor of Ely asserted that the region's population refused "to be pushed around any longer" by environmentalists. They were determined, he said, to defend their opportunities to use the canoe area for the economic and recreational values that mattered to them.

Irvin Anderson, a state representative from Minnesota, testified against both bills, arguing that Oberstar and Fraser accepted the authority of the federal government to control use of the area's water surface. Regarding Oberstar's bill, he claimed,

> The legislation pretends to acknowledge the state's ownership
> and jurisdiction over the waters of the BWCA but actually makes

a mockery of that acknowledgement by regulating or outright
banning of certain types of use of those waters. If the federal
government can tell us what we in Minnesota can or cannot do
on our public waters, then I submit that our ownership is mean-
ingless.[35]

He opposed both bills because they proposed eliminating travel on
certain water surface areas in the BWCA as a matter of federal statute. The representative viewed this as a clear infringement on the
state's right to regulate the use of navigable waters within its boundaries.[36]

Mathew Kaufman, president of the Boating Industry Associa-
tions, a trade group, testified in support of Oberstar's bill. He stated,
"There is a much greater need today for facilities providing various
types of recreational activity than there is for additional highly restricted wilderness areas."[37] Kaufman claimed that environmentalists
were in fact elitists who wanted to ban motor use on public lands in
the name of wilderness preservation. He argued that too many public
lands administered by the federal government were being closed for
use to all but a small minority:

> The preservationist has very strong ideas about who deserves to
> enjoy natural beauty. He would reserve enjoyment of our natural
> beauty for only those willing to hike, snowshoe, canoe, or climb
> to achieve it. This philosophy contends that the out-of-doors
> should be enjoyed in one way only, or not at all.[38]

Kaufman argued that most Americans preferred developed recreation
and that opportunities for such recreation should be provided by
federal land managers. He noted that U.S. Senator Frank Church had
supported a pro-motor policy in the Boundary Waters.[39]

Kaufman argued that Fraser's bill would discriminate against
elderly people and those with physical handicaps who wanted to visit
the area. He also cited two research reports that found that outboard
motors were "completely compatible with the aquatic environment."
Kaufman outlined technical improvements in engines that prevented
hydrocarbons from leaking into the water. He dismissed as self-serving research using opinion surveys which documented a conflict between visitors who did and did not use motors:

> The proposed ban of engine-powered boats seems to be based on
> ill-defined "conflicts" with other water-user groups. The real
> truth is that single-interest groups simply wish to have the "exclu-

sive" use of the BWCA's vast waterways for their own form of recreation, which they deem to be higher or more noble use than motorboating.[40]

Janet Green of the Duluth Audubon Society supported Fraser's bill at the subcommittee hearings. She argued that the management history of the canoe area was one of movement toward more restrictive rules to preserve the area. In her view, Oberstar's proposal for making part of the BWCA a national recreation area was a radical departure from this trend.[41] Green pointed to statistics that showed that recreationists who traveled by canoe had increased from less than 50 percent before 1960 to 72 percent by 1976. She maintained that other areas in the Superior National Forest and areas elsewhere in the region were open to motorized recreation. Green approached the issue from a philosophical standpoint, arguing that new social attitudes supported protecting natural areas:

> The Boundary Waters case is a classic example of the clash between ideologies typical of our time as we make the mental transition from a frontier attitude toward the land and its resources as unlimited to a land ethic attitude that allocates and manages limited resources with an eye to the future under principles of equity and reason. The setting aside of wilderness is an act of some humility by modern man.[42]

Timothy Knopp, a professor of forestry at the University of Minnesota, testified about conflicts between motor and nonmotor users in the canoe wilderness.[43] Because the irritation was one-sided, visitors who used motors were largely unable to appreciate the objections of those who traveled without them, he said. Motor users often dismissed visitors who chose not to use motors as selfish people who wanted to have an area only for themselves. Knopp observed, however, that the "means of access is itself a part of the environment and thus determines the kind of experience an area can provide."[44] He argued that visitors who wished to enter a natural area free from motor intrusions should have the opportunity to do so.

Knopp rejected the claim by Alliance supporters that motors helped to better distribute visitors in the canoe area and thereby reduced congestion problems. He argued that motors "only have the effect of making even the more remote areas appear crowded."[45] This was so, he said, because engine noises carried far, and the swift speed of motorboats meant increased contacts with other visitor parties. He asserted that "if motorized vehicles were permitted to enter all our

forests, everyone would be denied access to a machine-free environment." Knopp argued that under these circumstances "even the handicapped would be unable to find what many of them consider to be a
true wilderness experience."[46] He maintained that opening all public
lands to motorized recreation would deny a certain type of user a
chance to enjoy the outdoors in a preferred way.

William Muir, a botany instructor at Carleton College in Minnesota, also testified in support of Fraser's bill. He identified himself as
a severe diabetic requiring daily insulin shots. Muir, who also was
blind and needed special support shoes to walk, regularly visited the
canoe area without motorized assistance. He argued that his disabili-
ties did not prevent him from paddling and portaging in the Boundary
Waters wilderness. He criticized multiple-use supporters who argued
that Fraser's bill would discriminate against persons such as himself.
Muir called it a "phony issue, supported and perpetuated mainly by
those having little or no interest in the welfare of the handicapped."[47]
He noted that, if extended, the argument for using motors to allow
the handicapped access to the canoe area would require building
tramways to remote mountain peaks.

The Carter administration also introduced a proposal for managing the BWCA at the subcommittee hearings. This testimony, which
was a surprise for the Alliance and the Friends, was more in accord
with Fraser's bill than Oberstar's. The administration proposed to
increase the size of the wilderness area, to ban mining and logging,
and to prohibit most recreation that used motors. Secretary of Agriculture Robert Bergland stated that the proposal was

> consistent with the intent of President Carter to expand and im-
> prove our wilderness assets. It is a proposal that will help the
> people of Cook, Lake, and St. Louis counties to adjust to and
> capitalize on the changes under way in how people prefer to
> spend their leisure and money on outdoor recreation.[48]

Rudy Perpich, the governor of Minnesota, and his commissioner
of natural resources, William Nye, also testified at the hearings. They
supported a logging ban on the condition that alternative timber supplies be made available.[49] The state, however, wanted Congress to
allow continued motorized travel in the BWCA. Nye later elaborated
the state's position:

> The conflict between motorcraft use and paddle canoeists is pri-
> marily a recreational use question, and not an ecological ques-

tion. . . . There is room in the BWCA for controlled use of motorboats and canoes, cross-country skis and snowmobiles, all without significant ecological damage.[50]

Nye argued that motor-assisted recreation was firmly established in the area and that enforcing a complete ban would be impractical, as well as costly for resort owners. The commissioner, however, supported zoning parts of the area exclusively for nonmotor use.

Summary. The political conflict over motorized travel in the canoe area was a collision of two sets of values. The BWCA case is an example of a struggle between divergent social values over the role of technology in natural areas. This value conflict in the BWCA case suggests that differences between the two political coalitions were unresolvable. Russell Brown argues that in some political situations "conflict is inevitable and compromise is impossible."[51] Speaking of natural resource issues, Brown observes, "There are two incompatible ethical situations involved, one economic and the other aesthetic. Both are valid, but where they interact must, by their nature, conflict." This split in values, however, can in some cases be bridged. For example, as the recreational tastes of the public evolve toward appreciative values, outfitters and resorters can orient their services more toward marketing a wilderness experience. The result is that their businesses remain viable as economics is placed in the service of aesthetics.

In the Boundary Waters case, this meeting of economic and aesthetic values in a policy solution appeared impossible. The way in which the two sides framed the issues appeared to preclude the search for a policy that satisfied all interests. With respect to how humans should relate to the environment, S. F. Cotgrove observes,

> The protagonists face each other in a spirit of exasperation, talking past each other with mutual incomprehension. It is a dialogue of the blind talking to the deaf. Nor can the debate be settled by appeals to the facts. We need to grasp the implicit cultural meanings which underlie the dialogue.[52]

The gap in values between supporters and opponents of motorized recreation was too great to bridge through constructive dialogue.

Management of the canoe area was an issue that both sides felt intensely about, and a democratic political system, with its emphasis on compromise, usually fails to handle such situations well.

The anger of Alliance members toward environmentalists and the federal government reflected their concern over the impact of new legislation on their lives. Local supporters of multiple use strongly objected to defining motors as an inappropriate means to travel in the canoe area. The Friends certainly did not deny the need for some means of travel by water but argued that motorized travel should be excluded in the Boundary Waters. The motor was a symbol of advanced civilization, and wilderness enthusiasts wished to travel in the canoe country free from its intrusion. The political issue in question was what type of recreation BWCA visitors preferred. Developed campsites, aluminum canoes, and modern camping equipment did not appear to bother people who objected to motors. These artifacts were viewed as compatible with the search for a wilderness experience.

Whether a wooden paddle or an outboard motor is used to travel through the canoe area, technology is involved, and obvious advances have occurred in both types of water travel. Outboard motors have been designed to be more powerful and lighter in weight. Snowmobiles have changed from large and cumbersome machines to small sport models able to travel long distances in a short time. Canoes have also been made lighter, stronger, and more maneuverable. Advances in plastics and metals have resulted in better Nordic skis and camping gear for winter tours into the canoe wilderness. These improved technical designs have made wilderness travel possible for many people.

It was difficult for people who lived near the canoe area to understand visitors from outside the region *choosing* to travel without motors. This confusion can be partially explained by the different attitudes of people who live in urban and rural areas. Rural residents live where human artifacts are less concentrated, and they often rely on machines to lessen the effort required to complete tasks in the outdoors. Urban inhabitants live in a highly artificial world on a daily basis, and some desire a temporary escape to more natural surroundings. Not all urban residents, however, were opposed to motor use in the canoe area. As with all issues related to public land use, people sharing certain traits cannot be categorized as a group according to preference.

People who wanted to continue using motors in the border lakes wilderness did not accept the argument that Congress should ban motors to promote a wilderness experience for people who didn't think as they did. They saw this as an attempt by environmentalists to use the power of the federal government to define in a narrow way how the area could be enjoyed. Many residents resented the role of the Forest Service, and even the Congress, in deciding use priorities for the area. They saw these institutions as pawns used by preservation forces to achieve policy goals that were selfish and irrational.

Banning motors was viewed as selfish by Alliance members because they thought the area was large enough to support both forms of recreation. They argued that 40 percent of the water acreage was already reserved exclusively for canoeists and that the canoeists were free to share the remaining water surface in the BWCA with motorboat users. Some local people saw the environmentalists as elitists who tried to exclude another group from using the entire area. The multiple-use supporters generally could not accept the idea that motor and nonmotor forms of recreation were incompatible uses in the canoe wilderness area. They simply could not fathom the desire by canoeists to avoid motorized equipment.[53] Their outdoors experience was enhanced by using motors for travel in the wilderness. Moreover, they did not object to encounters with canoeists. Many local users viewed the means of travel as a matter of personal choice that should not be decided by the federal government.

A ban on motor use was seen as irrational by the Alliance because it seemed a waste of resources to set aside over one million acres of prime recreation area for the exclusive use of canoeists and skiers. Local users argued that the ban, imposed on them by outside forces, would harm the region's economy. Moreover, bans placed on snowmobile use in the winter would block the development of a potential winter tourism business, as at the present time the BWCA was seldom visited during the cold season. The multiple-use supporters believed that it should be managed for a range of recreation pursuits, including motor and nonmotor forms.

5 ❧ Congress Makes a Decision

The Burton-Vento Bill. After the September 1977 hearings in Washington, D.C., Phillip Burton's subcommittee drafted a new bill that included parts of the bills proposed by Oberstar, Fraser, and U.S. Secretary of Agriculture Robert Bergland. In February 1978 Burton and Bruce Vento, the U.S. representative from Saint Paul, revised the legislative proposal and introduced it on 16 March as H.R. 12250. It contained some concessions to multiple-use interests but clearly leaned toward the interests of wilderness advocates. The Burton-Vento bill proposed to increase the size of the area to 1,075,000 acres and to establish a national recreation area of 227,000 acres along the wilderness boundary lines as a buffer zone.[1] It banned all mining and logging, reduced motor use to fifteen peripheral lakes partly inside the wilderness boundaries, and allowed snowmobiles to cross the international border on two routes. The bill also authorized Congress to buy out resorts on certain lakes with motor bans and provided financial help for firms located on the edge of the wilderness to reorient their services to wilderness recreation.

The Friends' leaders saw the subcommittee bill as a compromise they could accept, although it fell short of banning all mechanized travel. A spokesman for the Wilderness Society supported H.R. 12250 but was concerned about the number of lakes still accessible by motor. David Zentner of the Izaak Walton League also approved of the bill as a fair means to resolve the dispute. He strongly supported its provisions for financial assistance to help edge firms adjust to the proposed management rules.[2]

The Alliance responded quite differently to H.R. 12250. Edward Zabinski, who had replaced Robert Buckler as the coalition's executive director, argued that the bill was "disastrous in terms of the local residents and everyone concerned with preserving the area as it is right now."[3] Alliance leaders did not find most of the bill's provisions acceptable and thus did not view it as a true compromise effort. They argued that the multiple-use side had lost nearly all the policy goals it wished to achieve. For them, H.R. 12250 was too heavily weighted in favor of wilderness interests to serve as a starting point for negotiations on a compromise bill.

The Alliance strongly opposed the bill's concept of the national recreation area. The group's leaders interpreted the provision as a threat to people who owned private property along the Echo, Fernberg, and Gunflint road corridors. They asserted that it would give authority to the secretary of agriculture to "condemn lands and property for any violation."[4] The Alliance objected to the creation of a 227,000-acre national recreation area, arguing that it threatened the right of citizens who owned private property in the proposed area to use it as they chose. The coalition also rejected the proposed motorboat and snowmobile restrictions in the BWCA and predicted severe economic dislocation if H.R. 12250 were approved. The group sided with the state government in its concern over the alleged loss of Minnesota's jurisdiction over water acreage in the canoe wilderness.[5]

Oberstar saw the Burton-Vento bill as a "false compromise" that did not represent a balancing of interests. Criticizing an editorial in a Duluth newspaper that supported H.R. 12250, he stated, "Your view of the bill appears to be based on the belief, or perhaps the wish, that because the motors and snowmobiles are not totally and absolutely banned from the BWCA the bill is a fair and reasonable compromise."[6] Oberstar contended that the two snowmobile trails into Ontario, Canada served as access routes for homeowners and were not for recreation. The congressman also claimed that the proposed cuts in motor use would damage the economic vigor of towns in the region and deprive a large group of people of their preferred mode of travel.

Alvin Hall, a Saint Louis county commissioner from Ely, stressed the idea that the Boundary Waters was in fact a semiwilderness area. This was the case, he argued, with respect to its long history of multiple use. Hall asserted that the Forest Service's dilemma was "having a congressional mandate to manage a recreation area under the 1964 Act while being increasingly shoved in the direction of pure wilderness by environmental lobbyists."[7] He charged that preservationists wanted the area for their exclusive use but had enough political tact to disguise their real aims behind words such as "protect, virgin timber, perpetuity, communing with nature, serenity, solitude, and undisturbed ecosystem." The county commissioner argued that the Friends used these words in an insidious manner that implied that local residents sought to destroy such values, which he said was not the case. Noting that motor use in the area caused no ecological damage, he asserted that "the only disturbance that exists is in the head of the sensitive canoe paddler." Hall objected to reserving one million acres of "extremely valuable recreation lands and waters to satisfy the inner needs of a few canoe paddlers, snowshoers, and cross-country skiers."

The Vermilion Lake Incident. A wilderness boundary line proposed in the Burton-Vento bill ignited a heated exchange over Vermilion Lake, a large lake west of Ely and mostly outside the Superior National Forest. The lake was near the towns of Tower and Soudan and included much private lakeshore development. The House subcommittee drew the new wilderness boundaries to include a small bay on the north end of Vermilion Lake. The bill provided that all peripheral lakes partially within the new boundaries would become wilderness lakes where motors, unless exempted by name, would be prohibited. The Alliance seized upon the inclusion of the small bay as an example of attempts by environmentalists to increase federal control over lands in northeastern Minnesota. Burton explained to the press that the subcommittee had never intended to make Vermilion Lake a wilderness lake. He had the map redrawn to exclude the inlet and correct the mistake. A state legislator, however, wanted the bill specifically amended to exclude the lake by name "because we've seen broken promises before."[8]

A few days later, Fraser attended a meeting on the issue of the boundary line in Cook, a town west of Vermilion Lake, at the Alliance's invitation. The environmentalists who went to the meeting described the atmosphere as "intimidating, uncivilized, and irrational."[9] A Friends supporter observed that multiple-use interests were "cruel and threatening to Fraser." Others claimed that the emotional climate at the Alliance meeting showed that residents of the Arrowhead communities were willing to fight for their side of the issue against the pressure of outside forces.

The Friends saw the Vermilion Lake incident as a calculated effort by the Alliance to increase its political support among people who lived in the region. The Friends' *Newsletter* commented,

> Wild claims that highly developed Lake Vermilion (and even far-off Pelican Lake) will be included in the wilderness are purveyed as truth throughout N.E. Minnesota. A considerable portion of this misinformation is perpetuated by the leaders of the Conservation Alliance (our organized opposition) and by the demagoguery of local politicians, in an effort to solidify local public opinion and gain financial support.[10]

A Duluth newspaper characterized the incident in the following manner: "There has been much heat and little light generated on this subject, because too many people have been misled to believe that the new bill would establish Lake Vermilion as a wilderness lake."[11] This bitter exchange showed the high level of political tension that had been reached over the question of how to manage the canoe area.

The disagreements over motor use in the BWCA continued to grow. An Alliance pamphlet argued that the basic views and interests of northeastern Minnesota communities were under attack: "The wilderness preservationists have depicted a conflict of values as a war between nature and its exploiters. They will not admit that nature can be enjoyed in different ways by different people."[12] The Alliance pointed out that although multiple uses in the border lakes had been established decades ago, this heritage was being "erased from human memory" to satisfy a purist ideal held by interests outside the region. As an example, the Alliance cited actions by Forest Service employees to dismantle cabins built by Finnish settlers. The Alliance asserted that wilderness partisans were not really concerned about actual environmental quality issues:

> Restricting public access to recreation areas does nothing to control pollutants or to protect resources. It is a tactic being used to

divert national attention from real environmental issues, with the support of major corporations. By calling themselves "environmentalists," the wilderness preservationists confuse their crusade with environmental issues.[13]

Increased Efforts by the Alliance. On 7 April 1978 the Alliance sponsored a dinner of wild game in Virginia, a town in the Arrowhead Region. It was held to raise money and political support for the multiple-use cause. The event was heavily attended and raised about 25,000 dollars; it also raised political expectations. U.S. Senator Wendell Anderson of Minnesota, told those who attended the dinner that he would "see to it that no bill gets to the Senate that the people of Minnesota cannot live with."[14] This pledge was received with great enthusiasm by the audience. Anderson was a member of the Senate Parks and Recreation Subcommittee, to which any BWCA bill passing the House of Representatives would be sent. This key position in Congress gave him important leverage in aiding the cause of protecting existing policies for motorized recreation. Anderson was in a strong position in the Senate to block attempts to pass any House bill that the Alliance objected to.

Other elected officials who spoke at the dinner told the audience that candidates for statewide office would need the support of the Arrowhead Region to be elected. Many Alliance members came away from the dinner flushed with excitement and hope for the future. It gave them a sense for the first time since the coalition had been formed that their goals were politically feasible. They began to think that the Alliance had the power base to shape the legislative process in a direction that promoted their interests. The event provided strong evidence of regional support for their policy goals, and it gave the Alliance statewide media exposure.

On 14 April 1978 the Alliance chapter in Cook County staged a protest at the Forest Service office building in Grand Marais. About one thousand residents turned out to demonstrate against the Burton-Vento bill. The Alliance protesters surrounded the building, cut off power and water, and placed a large wooden padlock on the front door.[15] The leaders of the demonstration then presented an eviction notice to Forest Service personnel, claiming that this symbolized the fate of people living in the area if H.R. 12250 became law. The Alliance directed the protest against the Forest Service because the secretary of agriculture had supported greater restrictions on motor use in the wilderness area. The Grand Marais protest again helped the Alliance capture crucial media attention throughout the state for its cause.

The protests and demonstrations organized by Alliance leaders spread to include actions in the Twin Cities area. On 3 June 1978 over twelve hundred supporters of the multiple-use cause arrived by bus in Saint Paul. They came to attend the state convention of the Democratic Farmer-Labor (DFL) Party.[16] The DFL party had convened to pick candidates to run on its ticket in the fall elections. Donald Fraser sought his party's endorsement as the candidate for the U.S. Senate. Alliance members picketed the entrance to the convention, carrying anti-Fraser signs that denounced the congressman for his positions on the Boundary Waters issues.

During the afternoon session, the protesters vented their hostility in a torrent of noise when Fraser appeared at the podium to address the convention. The uproar continued for several minutes until Oberstar appeared at the podium. He asked the crowd to let Fraser speak, and at this point the disruption ended and the mass of demonstrators turned and left the hall. Several DFL delegates who supported continued multiple use in the canoe area also walked out. By this orchestrated action, the Alliance visibly demonstrated the deep political split in the DFL party that the Boundary Waters issue had created.

During the convention, Douglas Johnson, a state senator from Cook, challenged Fraser for the U.S. Senate nomination to protest his position on the BWCA.[17] It took three ballots before Fraser received enough delegate votes to become the party's endorsed candidate. He had served the Fifth District in the U.S. House of Representatives for sixteen years and sought to fill the seat vacated by Senator Hubert Humphrey, who had died in January 1978. Senator Anderson, who as state governor had appointed himself to the senate when Walter Mondale became Carter's vice-president, won endorsement for the other seat on the first ballot. He did not face the same opposition that plagued Fraser at the convention.

The multiple-use supporters and antiabortion interests formed a coalition of delegates against Fraser for his policy stands at the Saint Paul convention. They were able to overturn a party resolution on the Boundary Waters that supported the Burton-Vento bill favored by Fraser. The DFL delegates had initially approved a plank in the state party platform calling for more restrictions on motorized recreation. This position, however, was reversed on a second vote engineered by Alliance leaders. The convention delegates who supported Wendell

Anderson launched an intensive lobbying effort on the floor against the antimotor resolution, and it was defeated.

The House Acts. The subcommittee chaired by Burton revised its controversial Boundary Waters bill to exclude the section creating a national recreation area and giving the federal government special zoning powers. Burton hoped that this change would dispel the fears of residents who owned real estate along the three major road systems bordering the canoe area. On 4 April 1978 the amended bill was passed by the subcommittee and sent to the House Committee on Interior and Insular Affairs, which was chaired by Morris Udall. He was ill at the time, so Burton presided over the full committee's deliberations on H.R. 12250. At this time, Oberstar presented another bill, which would ban logging but would retain current levels of motor use. His new bill also deleted the provision for making part of the BWCA a national recreation area, but it was rejected by the committee. On 10 April the full committee approved the Burton-Vento bill by a voice vote.

At this stage, wilderness supporters disagreed on the best strategy for passing H.R. 12250 on the House floor. Some leaders of the Friends argued that the BWCA bill had enough support to pass in its present form. Others thought that some concessions to multiple-use interests should be added to prevent Oberstar from offering amendments during the floor debate.[18] They pointed out that the legislation directly affected Oberstar's district and that some of his colleagues might be reluctant to vote against him. Other leaders of the Friends argued that some Republicans might vote for changes in H.R. 12250 in order to attack Fraser for his liberal stands on banning guns and allowing abortions.

The Friends agreed to write some multiple-use concessions into the Burton-Vento bill. Fraser and Vento drafted some amendments to weaken H.R. 12250 and sent them to Burton for his approval. Richard Nolan, a U.S. representative from the Sixth District in Minneapolis, helped write the changes. These compromises opened more lakes to motor use in the canoe wilderness. The Friends hoped that this increase in the water surface area open to motors would improve the chance for passage of H.R. 12250 before the Ninety-fifth Congress ended in October 1978. The bill was also altered to create a mining protection area of 222,000 acres along the three road corridors of the border lakes. This alteration, which banned mining unless a national emergency arose, added protection for recreational values.

The Alliance remained dissatisfied with H.R. 12250, even with the changes. Oberstar called them "cosmetic surgery" and a weak attempt by wilderness interests to reach a political compromise.[19] Miron Heinselman, the Friends' chairman, saw the bill's changes in a different way. He did not like them but agreed that they were needed to improve the chances of getting a BWCA wilderness bill passed during the current session.[20] The amended bill fell short of the coalition's goals for a total wilderness, but most members accepted the changes because they believed that the basic principle of preserving the wilderness area remained intact.

On 5 June 1978 the House of Representatives voted on H.R. 12250 after a two-hour floor debate. Vento explained that while drafting the bill the national parks subcommittee had studied four issues: mining, logging, motorboating, and snowmobiling. Both sides in the dispute had agreed to ban mining and logging after reaching agreements acceptable to both. The remaining issue concerned motorized access to the canoe area. The subcommittee had decided to accept the secretary of agriculture's view that snowmobile use should continue on two routes into Ontario. Vento argued that the motorboat issue centered on three facts. First, paddle-only canoe use was the "predominant form" of BWCA recreation used by BWCA visitors.[21] Second, conflict between visitors who did and those who did not use motors had been documented in opinion survey research. Third, "motor use has historically been considered incompatible with wilderness designation by Congress." Vento argued that compromises in the wilderness bill to allow some motor use would protect local interests.

Oberstar attacked H.R. 12250 as "an abrogation of the promises and assurances made to the people of northern Minnesota."[22] He referred to section 4 (d)(5) of the Wilderness Act of 1964, which stated that established motorboat use was to continue. Oberstar asserted that Congress in its vote on H.R. 12250 had to decide whether to "abide by these assurances or to state that they no longer applied." He argued that the exemption clause in the 1964 statute recognized the unique semiwilderness character of the border lakes canoe area. Oberstar quoted a letter from Rupert Cutler, the assistant secretary of agriculture, stating that motor use at current levels did not lower the water quality of the border lakes.[23] He stressed that motors did not cause ecological disruption but that H.R. 12250 would disrupt and harm the local economy. Other colleagues rose to support Oberstar's views, but the Burton-Vento bill was approved by a vote of 324 to 29.

Senate Politics. On 23 June Senators Wendell Anderson and Muriel Humphrey introduced a Boundary Waters bill, S. 3242, in the Senate. The provisions in this bill on mining and logging were the same as those in H.R. 12250. The Anderson-Humphrey bill, however, differed sharply from the House bill in regard to motorboat and snowmobile use. It provided that 58 percent of the water surface in the wilderness area remain open for motorboat use, a figure just slightly under the existing level of 62 percent. The bill also permitted snowmobiles on eight of the most popular routes in use prior to the 1976 ban imposed by the secretary of agriculture. The provisions for motorized recreation were the same as those written into Oberstar's final BWCA bill. In introducing S. 3242 on the Senate floor, Anderson stated that it would "continue to permit local residents, resorters, tourists, the elderly, or the non-canoeists to use the beautiful lakes of the BWCA to do a little fishing during the day."[24]

Anderson held a news conference in Duluth just before introducing the bill in the Senate. He argued that wilderness supporters must be willing to compromise with motor interests. If the gap between S. 3242 and H.R. 12250 could not be closed, he stated, it was unlikely that the Ninety-fifth Congress would pass a bill. Edward Zabinski, the Alliance's executive director, called Anderson's bill a "constructive proposal." It was close to the type of bill that Alliance members and Oberstar wished to see passed. But a spokesman for the Wilderness Society argued that S. 3242 was "unrealistic" as a starting point for negotiations.[25] Leaders of the Friends also concluded that it was "unacceptable to the environmental community and to the majority of BWCA users who desire a quiet nonmechanized wilderness."

As a member of the Subcommittee on Parks and Recreation, Anderson arranged a field trip to the canoe area to give his colleagues a closer view of the issue. On 17 July 1978 six senators arrived in Ely, including James Abourezk from North Dakota, who chaired the subcommittee. Dale Bumpers from Arkansas, Howard Metzenbaum from Ohio, Gaylord Nelson from Wisconsin, and the two Minnesota senators came on the field trip. They spent the first day listening to the Alliance and the Friends present their positions. On the second

day the senators toured parts of the border lakes, traveling by motorboat, floatplane, and canoe.

One Alliance spokesman who resided in Ely made several points
in a presentation to the senators. As a former Forest Service em-
ployee, he argued that management of the border lakes was too "often influenced by professional environmental groups rather than by
professional foresters."[26] He maintained that the basic issue was "simply one involving personal choice," as travel by motors did no ecological damage. The basic idea stressed by the Alliance spokesman was
that "the primitive character of the BWCA must be maintained, but
without unnecessary restrictions on motor use."[27]

Another Alliance member pointed out that the BWCA, in the
strict use of the term, was not a wilderness. The area had a long
history of human use, he said, and labeling it as primitive did not
make it so. He stated that antimotor interests hoped to use the legislative process to establish a wilderness by "political demarcation."[28] The
Alliance representative argued that technological advances in watercraft, such as aluminum boats and outboard motors, "saved time
and labor." He pointed out that American Indians on both sides of the
international border had adopted these improvements, noting that
"the values of today's recreational canoeists are a recent phenome-
non."[29] He associated these values with "a sport of urban people" who
wanted to find adventure and "test their endurance against nature."
He argued, however, that other BWCA visitors had different values in
that they did "not believe that motors are incompatible with the surroundings."

The Dayton-Walls Compromise. At the end of the subcommittee field trip, Senator Abourezk asked the two coalitions to sit down
with each other and attempt to resolve the conflict over motor use.
The subcommittee chairman pointed out the advantage of a compromise. Members of both groups had a detailed grasp of the geography
of the area and were knowledgeable about the issues of resource use.
An agreement between the two coalitions, Abourezk believed, would
likely result in a better statute for each than one imposed by Congress. Abourezk proposed that the two groups meet in Washington,
D.C. to negotiate an agreement with his staff aide, who would act as a
mediator.

The leaders of both coalitions had little hope that an attempt at mediation would resolve their differences. Both sides believed they had given enough. They agreed, however, to send a representative to the meeting. The Friends chose Charles Dayton, an attorney from Minneapolis, to represent them, and the Alliance picked Ronald Walls, an attorney from Ely. Any agreements the two men reached were to be presented to their respective groups for formal approval or rejection. Joseph Alexander, commissioner of Minnesota's Department of Natural Resources, expressed anger at the Senate plan to negotiate a solution to the impasse.[30] The state had not been invited to send a representative to the meetings, although, he argued, it had a clear stake in any policy outcome. The state government owned land in the federal wilderness boundaries, and it also sought to retain jurisdiction over rights for water surface use.

On 28 July Dayton and Walls began negotiations on where motors should be allowed in the BWCA, for what period of time, and with what power level. The meetings went on for three days, with a final session on 30 July lasting all night. The two men agreed to reduce the water area for motorboat use from 58 to 33 percent and to phase out the area for outboard motor use to 24 percent by 1999. The agreement, however, allowed permanent access for motorized vehicles to several large lakes for which access had been banned by H.R. 12250. It also reduced snowmobile travel to five routes, with the stipulation that in January 1984 only two routes that crossed into Canada would remain open.

Dayton and Walls returned to Minnesota to explain the technical points of the agreement to the leaders of their coalitions. Members of the Friends crowded into Miron Heinselman's home in Saint Paul for an executive committee meeting. As Dayton was explaining the compromise — but before Friends leaders could vote to accept or reject the agreement — word reached them from a newspaper reporter that the Alliance was overwhelmingly opposed to the agreement. The Alliance chapter in Ely, by a unanimous vote of its 201 members, rejected the Dayton-Walls compromise. Alliance members of the Grand Marais chapter voted 101 to 13 against it.[31] The news of this event made any further discussion of the terms of the agreement by the Friends moot. The failure of the Dayton-Walls compromise to resolve the impasse cast in doubt the possibility that Congress could pass a BWCA bill before the session ended. It also marked a distinct political setback for Senator Anderson, who hoped that the negotiations he had helped to arrange would resolve the dispute.

The Alliance's swift rejection of the compromise enhanced the public image of the Friends. The Friends gained political capital because many people saw the group as more reasonable and conciliatory than the other side. The Alliance contended, however, that its policy goals had been hacked to pieces in the Washington, D.C. meetings. Alliance President Lenore Johnson, who was from Two Harbors, characterized the results of the negotiations as unworthy of further discussion. She stated that the present Alliance strategy was to block passage of any bill in the last weeks of the Ninety-fifth Congress. Oberstar told Alliance activists that he believed that the chances were better for passing a multiple-use Boundary Waters bill during the next legislative session.[32] He thought that the candidates for Congress who supported bans on motors, which were unpopular locally, would pay for their views during the November 1978 elections.

The Battle Ends. Soon after the negotiations in Washington, D.C. the Senate subcommittee began drafting a bill based on H.R. 12250 and agreements reached in the Dayton-Walls compromise. This was a red flag for Alliance members, who had made their negative views on the compromise known in unmistakable terms. On 5 August, responding to Anderson's decision to incorporate the agreement reached between Dayton and Walls into the Senate BWCA bill, the Alliance set up roadblocks around the Ely area. Members of the group stopped visitors wishing to enter or leave the canoe wilderness, and this led to verbal abuse on both sides. Rather than presenting the Alliance's concerns in a favorable light, the roadblock protest appeared only to make the general public resent the group's tactics.

Some Alliance supporters argued that Vice President Walter Mondale had pressured Anderson into supporting the new Senate bill. But an aide to the vice president denied that Mondale had anything to do with the turn of events, although the Carter administration supported greater motor use restrictions.[33] Other residents who lived near the canoe area and multiple-use supporters directly blamed Anderson for the new subcommittee bill. The senator knew that both the Alliance and Representative Oberstar rejected the Dayton-Walls compromise in emphatic terms, yet he insisted on pushing it forward. Anderson chaired a subcommittee hearing in Washington, D.C. on 17 August, and Assistant Secretary of Agriculture Rupert Cutler testified in support of the Senate bill that included the Dayton-Walls compromise.[34] This endorsement by the Carter administration moved the proposal closer to passage.

On 26 September 1978 the Senate subcommittee completed work on its amendments to H.R. 12250. Getting the bill passed and to the president's desk for his signature was jeopardized by two factors. First, as was always the case near the end of its sessions, Congress had to consider a large number of bills in a short period of time. Second, those who supported continued motor use argued that Fraser's defeat to Robert Short as the DFL Senate candidate in the state primaries was a result of his unpopular positions on BWCA issues. The Alliance tried to increase its political leverage in Congress by pointing to Fraser's defeat.

On 3 October the Senate Committee on Energy and Natural Resources, chaired by Henry Jackson of Washington, discussed and approved Anderson's bill. It was introduced on the Senate floor on 9 October and late in the night passed without any debate. The ease with which the bill was approved by the Senate was galling to the Alliance leaders. This was the point at which pro-motor supporters had hoped to block the Fraser version of a Boundary Waters bill. The H.R. 12250 version of the Senate bill then went back to the House, where Burton and Vento worked to get the Dayton-Walls compromise embodied in the bill accepted by their colleagues. On 11 October the members of a conference committee met to discuss the House and Senate versions of the BWCA bill. The House members agreed to accept the details of H.R. 12250 as amended by the Senate.

The bill reached the House floor for debate and a vote on the morning of 14 October, the last day of the Ninety-fifth Congress. Oberstar urged his colleagues to vote against the bill, calling it a "monstrous outrage" against the people in his district.[35] He asked the House to take up a new bill in the next session of Congress to avoid the "high tension politics that swirl around this deeply divisive issue." Rising to support Oberstar, Steven Symms, a representative from Idaho, called the bill a coercive measure. He argued that H.R. 12250 was written to push "legislation down the throat of the people of Minnesota."[36]

Fraser argued that neither his defeat in the primaries nor the highly charged atmosphere of the issue was reason enough for the House to reject the bill in the last hours of the session. He urged his colleagues to view the federally owned canoe area as a truly national resource. Fraser also cited statewide opinion surveys showing that a majority of Minnesota citizens favored tighter restrictions on motor use.[37] The House passed H.R. 12250 by a wide margin of 248 to 111, and before the Ninety-fifth Congress ended, the Senate passed the same bill during the last hour of the session. Despite Oberstar's request that he not do so, President Carter signed the Boundary Waters Canoe Area Wilderness Act (P.L. 95-495) into law on 21 October 1978.

Summary. The controversy over whether motors should be permitted in the Boundary Waters for recreation ended with a compromise tilted in favor of the Friends. In passing P.L. 95-495, Congress had reduced motor use to nearly half the water surface area allowed by Secretary Freeman's regulations of 1965. It provided for decreases in motorboat use, from 62 to 24 percent of the BWCA's water surface area by 1999, and allowed only two permanent snowmobile routes into Canada to remain open. The statute included provisions for financial assistance to help outfitters and resorters adjust their operations to the new resource use rules.

Through intense efforts to shape the outcome of the policy process, each side tried to get its values embodied in a new statute. The conflict over whether motorized or nonmotorized travel should have priority in the canoe area reflected a division in thought about relations between humans and nature. The Alliance stressed the practicality of using motors to travel with greater speed and ease. This was especially so for many residents, who used their free time on weekends to make short trips into the canoe wilderness. The coalition stressed that section 4 (d)(5) of the Wilderness Act of 1964 had promised northeastern Minnesota residents the continued use of established motor routes. Alliance supporters did not push for increased motor use but for retaining existing levels.

Members of the Alliance argued that the use of motorized transportation was a matter of personal choice. They remained unresponsive to the complaints by canoeists that motors disturbed their enjoyment of the wilderness area. The complaints of the canoeists were viewed as a subjective matter of individual taste, and thus as a poor reason in itself for banning motors. Many residents believed they were being asked to set aside their recreational preferences so that outsiders could have their particular version of a wilderness experience. This galled many Alliance members, who pointed to the economic sacrifices they would be required to make.

The Friends sought legislation to make the Boundary Waters area free of all motor use. They wanted to achieve a sense of isolation from modern civilization, which was disturbed by encounters with motors. The Friends viewed mechanized recreation as incompatible with the wilderness. They wished to ban motors only on the one million acres inside the canoe area boundaries, not on the other two million acres of the Superior National Forest. The canoe area contained the best terrain for canoeing in the entire nation. They wanted to establish a public policy that excluded motors and other uses that diminished the wilderness qualities of the region.

There were several reasons for the decision by Congress to enact P.L. 95-495. One was that the policy to further reduce motor travel was the result of conflict in a pluralist political system in which one group of interests proved stronger than the other. Another reason, closely related to the pluralist explanation, was that legislators in strategic positions were able to shape the policy outcome. Lastly, mandated reductions in motor use can be viewed as the result of an ongoing transition in American attitudes toward the natural environment. This transition can be viewed in the context of the pluralist political system, in that policy changes in national priorities are to some extent brought about by value changes in American culture.

The Friends had an advantage over the Alliance in that many of its leaders had fought preservationist battles before in the national political arena. They had gained useful political skills by working with the Sierra Club, Audubon Society, Izaak Walton League, and other environmental groups. Members of these groups belonged to the Friends coalition, and they applied their expertise in lobbying efforts to ban motors in the canoe area. The Friends coalition was formed expressly to avoid competition between various national environmental groups that might have created discord by insisting on pushing their particular doctrines and strategies. In contrast, most Alliance leaders lacked experience in national politics and had never been involved in attempts to shape public policy at the federal level. Their efforts were often based on trial and error.

The Alliance was also at a disadvantage because it was formed a full year after the Friends coalition was established. In fact, the Alliance was organized in response to the growing success of the Friends. Alliance members, who favored Oberstar's bill, organized relatively late because many residents argued that current management policies should be left in place. Alliance members were also slow to realize the extent of the threat to the way they wished the area to be managed. By the time enough people favoring multiple-use recreation realized that they needed to organize, much political momentum had been lost to the group's opponents.

The Friends, unlike the Alliance, had a highly focused policy goal at the outset. The former were committed to a wilderness policy that eliminated all uses but primitive recreation, and they worked steadily to achieve this goal. In contrast, groups in the Alliance coalition had a variety of goals; each group thought that its particular goals should be the primary focus of the organization. Snowmobilers, motorboaters, resort owners, outfitters, loggers, and area business owners all tended to view managing the Boundary Waters from their respective points of view.[38] These groups learned to work together more effectively as time passed, but their consolidated efforts came too late in the policy process to turn things in their favor.

The Friends had another advantage in that their policy positions were explained to the media by only a few spokesmen. The Alliance had too many individuals who claimed to represent its views making statements to the press. These positions sometimes contradicted one another, and this damaged the coalition's public image.[39] A lack of editorial support for the Alliance in the Twin Cities' newspapers also hindered its political efforts.

A last advantage was logic. Most people found it illogical to allow motorized forms of travel in the Boundary Waters if it was to be a wilderness area. Motorized travel and wilderness were contradictory ideas. Although the Friends had no objection to sharing the area, the group did object to the use of motors because they violated the serenity of the wilderness. The environmentalists believed it was impossible to have wilderness and motorized recreation in the same area.

The Alliance did possess two advantages, but neither was able to change the policy outcome in 1978. First, the group was engaged in defending existing resource uses in the area. In the American political system, efforts to alter rather than retain policies are usually more difficult. Second, the Alliance supported bills sponsored by James Oberstar, who represented the Eighth District, in which the BWCA was located. Members of Congress often resist voting against a colleague when a measure he or she supports directly concerns his or her district.

If legislators in key positions had opposed new motor bans the policy outcome might have been quite different. For example, had Senator Humphrey been active during the last stages of the policy process, decreases in motor use might not have occurred, at least to the extent they did. Given his role in writing section 4 (d)(5) of the Wilderness Act of 1964, his personal influence might have been sufficient to retain existing levels of motor use. Thus, Humphrey's poor health and subsequent death from cancer in January 1978 can be seen as a major factor in determining the outcome of provisions in the 1978 act.

This explanation for how the 1978 statute came into being is also supported by a look at legislative action on the subcommittee level. As chairman of the House Subcommittee on Parks and Insular Affairs, Representative Phillip Burton was in a position to write a bill which he wanted to have passed. Burton had a clear record for supporting environmental causes over the years. Had Representative Steven Symms of Idaho chaired the subcommittee, then quite a different decision might have been made. Symms was well known for his opposition to the designation of federal lands as wilderness areas, and he was a strong supporter of states rights. During floor debate on H.R. 12250, Symms had strongly opposed more restrictions on motor use in the canoe area.

Senator Wendell Anderson, a member of the Senate Subcommittee on Parks and Recreation, was in an excellent position to shape a bill on motorized recreation levels. He almost certainly could have achieved more concessions for motor interests, and he might have even prevented any bill from passing the Ninety-fifth Congress. For any of several reasons, some of which are probably known only to himself, Anderson decided to support the Dayton-Walls compromise as an amendment to H.R. 12250. Had he rejected this compromise and promoted the interests of the Alliance, P.L. 95-495 as it exists would probably not have passed.

The mandated decrease in motor use may also be explained as a result of a gradual change in social attitudes toward the environment. At an earlier point in history, Americans generally believed in applying new forms of technology wherever possible to manage nature. With the rise of the environmental movement, more Americans began to believe that technology should be applied in a selective manner. Preserving wild lands is a good example of this new approach to the natural world. It is technically possible to build roads into the border lakes region and to use floatplanes, motorboats, and snowmobiles for faster and easier travel. Environmentalists, however, see such methods of travel as incompatible with a wilderness ethic.[40]

All of the above reasons help account for the 1978 decision to decrease travel by motors. The interested public and elected officials appeared persuaded more by the arguments of the Friends than those of the Alliance. According to opinion surveys conducted in Minnesota, most citizens viewed motor travel as incompatible with the wilderness. The Friends coalition was able to organize and promote its policy goals more effectively than its opposition, in part because public attitudes already leaned toward its views. The coalition was also able to build more support in Congress and the Carter adminis- tration because it had supporters in strategic positions. In addition, a wilderness area without motors was an idea whose time had come, and its success was pushed along by the rise of new cultural values.

6 ᶜ⦣ A New Statute and Adjustments

Reactions in the Arrowhead Region. Alliance members were dismayed both by the process and the outcome of the policy decision reached by Congress. Many northeastern Minnesota residents were angry with Senator Anderson because he had reversed the position taken earlier at the Virginia wild-game dinner in April 1978. Rather than working to block the Burton-Vento bill with the influence he held, Anderson had supported concessions to the Friends, which were embodied in the Dayton-Walls compromise. He decided to support the Dayton-Walls compromise, against the explicit wishes of the Alliance. Edward Zabinski, the executive director of the Alliance, argued that P.L. 95-495 was a defeat for the democratic process, as the legislation was very unpopular in the region.[1]

On 16 October 1978, during Senator Edward Kennedy's visit to Duluth on behalf of Anderson's campaign, some Alliance protesters surrounded the car the politicians were riding in and jeered Anderson.[2] This was one expression of the sense of betrayal many local people felt by the outcome of the policy process. Alliance leaders claimed the new law threatened their economic interests and rights as citizens who owned private property. These were two very different arguments, and those who opposed the 1978 statute would use both to attack it. Anderson lost in the November elections to his Republican challenger; the Alliance attributed his defeat to the role he had played in helping to pass the BWCA Wilderness Act.

One Ely resident's reaction to the statute expressed well the frustration felt by many residents who lived near the canoe area. He saw environmentalists as "powerful groups across this land so bent on locking up forests as playgrounds they forget people who earn a living on that land."[3] The man viewed wild and scenic river proposals and plans for a zone to protect wolves in northern Minnesota as more attempts to "grab" land. He was concerned about the possibility of government buyouts of private lands and additional constraints on resource use in the name of protecting nature. Anger at the legislative process and fear about the outcome created the political climate needed to challenge P.L. 95-495.

On 8 December 1978 the newly elected Republican governor, Albert Quie, met with Alliance leaders in Saint Paul to discuss P.L. 95-495. They discussed the new restrictions on motor use in the canoe area and general concerns over the amount of land owned by the federal government in northern Minnesota. Zabinski and other leaders of the Alliance suggested that the governor direct his attorney general to file a lawsuit to prevent the Forest Service from implementing the statutory bans on motors. The governor initially opposed litigation, believing that Congress was the proper institution to seek changes in management of the border lakes. But he was open to their grievances, noting that "people are just plain upset with government coercing them."[4]

The Ely-Winton Alliance. In January 1979 members of the Ely chapter of the Alliance voted to incorporate themselves into the Ely-Winton Alliance. Other chapters of the Alliance had become inactive, and the members drifted apart after the legislative struggle ended. The members in the Ely area, however, wanted to continue the fight. They refused to accept the new statute as legitimate and wanted to overturn it. They also voted to join the National Association of Property Owners (NAPO), a citizen interest group based in Texas. NAPO's goal was to protect private property rights against alleged abuses by government officials.

In April 1979 Ben Wallis, a NAPO attorney, asserted at an Ely-Winton Alliance meeting that the federal government's policy was to "acquire as much land as they could, and to take as much land out of production as possible."[5] While not making a legal argument, he noted that private property was a deeply rooted social value in the Judeo-Christian tradition. Wallis cited the biblical injunction that men should subdue the earth and have dominion over all living creatures.[6] He argued that America was founded on the property rights of individuals and that private land ownership was essential to a free society.

Wallis told the Ely group that it would need a sizable amount of money to challenge the constitutionality of certain provisions in the new Boundary Waters statute. He recommended that the Alliance seek a temporary injunction to block implementation of the law until the legal issues were decided. As the state of Minnesota had not yet filed a suit against the federal government, he suggested that the group sue Governor Quie. The lawsuit would charge him with failing to discharge his responsibility as a state official. Wallis admitted, however, that the latter action would do little more than publicize the group's discontent, as there were no legal arguments to force the state government to litigate the issue. The Alliance wanted the state to file suit so that the group would not have to bear all the attorney fees.

The State Decides. In March 1979 two assistant attorney generals sent a memorandum to Joseph Alexander, the commissioner of the State Department of Natural Resources. They cited *U.S. v. Brown,* a court case involving the right of the federal government to regulate hunting on state-owned waters in Voyageurs National Park.[7] The federal district court had ruled that the property clause in the Constitution "authorized federal regulation of hunting on state owned lakes."[8] The court reasoned that hunting interfered with the purpose for which Congress had established the Voyageurs National Park. The lower court decision was upheld on appeal. The memorandum advised against filing a suit to overturn the statutory restrictions on motorized travel, arguing that it had little chance of success.

On 17 April Commissioner Alexander, however, confirmed to the press that the state would proceed with a lawsuit. He asserted that the federal government did not have the constitutional right to regulate the use of state-owned waters and that it was thus important to resist efforts to extend further control over the wilderness area by the federal government. Alexander pointed out that the state's role in managing the area was vital to protecting its wilderness qualities.[9] He noted that the state and the Izaak Walton League had opposed the mining attempts by George St. Clair, without the support of the federal government.[10] The commissioner contended that in the future federal officials might decide to permit mining, which Minnesota, with its loss of water rights, would not be able to prevent.

The state's decision to sue the federal government was sharply criticized by the Friends' leaders, who argued that it was against the state's interests. A newspaper editorial asserted that that court action would result in more battles between interest groups and waste state tax dollars. The editorial argued that the decision by Governor Quie to sue the federal government was a payoff to satisfy political interests in the Arrowhead Region. It noted that the governor's "heart really does lie with those who see no special value in a canoe wilderness."[11] The editorial suggested that Quie at heart was a multiple-use proponent. Another editorial argued that litigation might result in the delay or cancellation of funds appropriated by Congress to implement the statute.[12]

A Duluth newspaper pointed out that the state should attempt to resolve its differences with the Forest Service by helping to write rules for implementing P.L. 95-495. If this failed to satisfy the state's interests, the editorial said, only then should the state consider court action. The editorial noted that the new law did not eliminate state control over water routes as long as the "state imposed regulations on motors at least as stringent as regulations proposed by the Forest Service."[13] It claimed that Congress had not "arbitrarily taken away the state's jurisdiction over BWCA waters" but had "simply set up conditions the state must meet if it wants to maintain that local jurisdiction." The editorial argued that rather than challenging the law, multiple-use supporters should work to get appropriations from the federal government.

The Alliance Files Suit. At the Ely-Winton Alliance's June 1979 meeting in Duluth, NAPO attorney Ben Wallis stressed that local interests needed to remain unified in opposing the new law. Wallis attacked the purist concept of nature: "Too many people in the country don't really know what the wilderness movement is all about. There are people in this state who still think wilderness is something you can drive your family up to on a weekend and get out and enjoy."[14] He claimed there was "no place for man in the true wilderness philosophy." Wallis argued that the law denied most people access to the Boundary Waters. Summing up the group's concerns, a brochure put out by the Ely-Winton Alliance stated:

> What is at stake is the right of a State to manage its own waters, the citizen's right to own property, the freedom to choose where one will live without fear of condemnation, the right of every individual to have the opportunity to experience the uniqueness of the area without discrimination.[15]

On 13 July 1979 the Alliance and other interested parties filed suit against the secretary of agriculture in District Court for the District of Columbia. The plaintiffs alleged that the 1978 act was a violation of private property rights protected by the U.S. Constitution. They asked the court to issue an injunction to prevent implementation of the law until the legal merits of the case had been determined.

Several affidavits were filed to support the court action. Frank Salerno, an Alliance leader and Ely realtor, stated that P.L. 95-495 threatened the economic interests and property rights of local people.[16] He objected to the right of first refusal, which gave the federal government the first option to buy property offered for sale by resort owners on lakes specified in the statute. He argued that the right of first refusal violated the freedom of resort owners to sell their property in the manner they chose.

Louise Leoni, a Saint Louis County tax assessor, argued that "the consequence of this legislation is that many properties are virtually unmarketable, and many sell for less than what a true market value should be."[17] She declared that a decline in local property values was the result of a "cloud of government intervention" by which buyers and sellers were forced to make decisions in uncertain market conditions. Leoni argued that P.L. 95-495 was creating the conditions for economic stagnation and decline.

Leoni also contended that the 1978 act would erode the local tax base. The motor restrictions would force some resort owners, who could not make enough money to stay in business, to sell their property to the government, increasing the tax burden on area homeowners. She also objected to the new BWCA visitor quotas imposed by the Forest Service, arguing that they ended "any hope of increased revenues from increased tourism." In her affidavit, Leoni stated that the interests who had helped to pass P.L. 95-495 ignored the "economic chaos" caused by the statute.

Leoni criticized supporters of the 1978 law for refusing to accept that local people were as much a part of the ecology of the canoe area as trees and other natural objects. This refusal angered residents, many of whom had lived in the Arrowhead Region their entire lives and were accustomed to using motorboats and snowmobiles to travel in the canoe area. The Boundary Waters was not an untouched or pristine wilderness area but one in which a clear tradition of human use had become established. The local population in many cases felt it was being branded as undesirable users and was being forced out of the area. The residents viewed themselves as an integral part of the lakes and forests of the BWCA.

Steve Jourdain, chief of the Lac La Croix Indian Reservation in Ontario, Canada, also filed an affidavit with the court. He argued that his village needed to use outboard motors for guiding clients into the border lakes region on hunting and fishing trips. Jourdain stated, "Since both parks are now under the new wilderness craze, we now have the parks in our backyards, but cannot use them."[18] He argued that guiding services provided a way for the tribe to earn a living.

The federal attorneys who defended P.L. 95-495 argued that the statute was a "valid exercise of congressional authority."[19] Charles Dayton, who represented the Sierra Club at a hearing before Judge Harold Greene's district court, argued against the restraining order sought by the plaintiffs, who had requested that the statute not be implemented until the legal questions were settled through the judicial process. Dayton pointed out that the restraining order could reopen the canoe area to the logging or mining allowed under the old management plan. He said it might also confuse people who were planning to visit the wilderness for recreation about what uses were now allowed. Although plaintiffs connected the loss in tourist trade in

1979 with the new law, Dayton noted that it could be explained as
easily by the national gas shortage.[20] On 17 July 1979 Judge Greene
denied the request by the plaintiffs for an injunction against the 1978
act. He ruled that there were no legal grounds for issuing an order to
delay implementing the statute.

The Lawsuit Refiled. The Ely-Winton Alliance, angry with the
court's decision, claimed that the hearing in the courtroom revealed
an improper relationship between the Forest Service and the Sierra
Club.[21] The plaintiffs asked Representative Oberstar to investigate
these charges, but he failed to find any evidence to support them.
Wallis withdrew *NAPO v. U.S.* from Judge Greene's court and refiled
it in Federal District Court in Duluth. In October 1979 the plaintiffs
asked the court to delay making a decision until the State of Minnesota had filed a lawsuit, because it was likely that the two cases would
be heard together.

On 21 December 1979 Commissioner Alexander, acting for the
state government, filed a lawsuit against Secretary of Agriculture
Robert Bergland. *Minnesota v. Bergland* challenged section 4 of P.L.
95-495, which placed restrictions on motor travel in the border lakes.
The state alleged that this provision violated its right to determine use
of the water surface within the boundaries of the wilderness area. In a
newspaper article Alexander was quoted as saying,

> For the first time in the BWCA's history, the federal government
> is attempting to establish regulations restricting the use of state
> waters in the area. Federal authority in the wilderness areas has
> always been limited to federal lands . . . water regulation has
> been left to the state.[22]

Brian O'Neill, a Minneapolis attorney who represented the defendants, challenged the state's professed motives for bringing the lawsuit. He asserted, "Statements about the state's traditional rights over
water bodies . . . are simply intended to hide the fact that this lawsuit
is about snowmobiles and motorboats."[23] O'Neill claimed the real
purpose of the state's lawsuit was to restore motor travel in the canoe
area.

In January 1980 NAPO and other parties filed a second lawsuit
in district court in Duluth against the federal government. In *NAPO*

v. Bergland, the plaintiffs alleged that the secretary of agriculture had "failed to file environmental impact statements prior to requests for appropriations from Congress to implement the Act."[24] They asked the court to prevent the secretary from administering the statute until an impact statement had been written. On 27 March 1980 the plaintiffs asked that the three cases be combined and heard together in district court. The request was granted, and Judge Miles Lord heard arguments from plaintiffs and defendants on 2 May.

The District Court Decision. On 24 July 1980 Judge Lord ruled against the plaintiffs in *NAPO v. U.S.* and *Minnesota v. Bergland.* He dismissed *NAPO v. Bergland* on the ground that the plaintiffs had failed to state a claim for relief.[25] His decisions were summarized in an opinion that combined the cases. The plaintiffs in *NAPO v. U.S.* had argued, among other points, that restrictions on motor use violated their Fifth and Ninth amendment rights to personal freedom and due process of law. Lord ruled that the right to travel in the area by motor did not rise to the level of fundamental rights guaranteed in the Constitution. The judge also ruled that banning the use of snowmobiles and motorboats did not violate the right of plaintiffs to due process of law. The plaintiffs had argued that their rights "to own, use, control, and dispose of their property" had been unconstitutionally restricted.[26]

Lord also rejected the claim that P.L. 95-495 violated the Webster-Ashburton Treaty of 1842, which stated that lakes on the international boundary would remain "free and open to the use of citizens" of both countries.[27] Lord ruled that the treaty did not prevent the two governments from regulating the use of waters bisected by international boundaries. He held that visitors could still travel across these lakes with paddle canoes without motor assistance.

The Alliance and other plaintiffs had also challenged section 5 (b) of the 1978 act as arbitrary and capricious. That section allowed owners of resorts on certain lakes who sold their property to the federal government to retain up to three acres for their personal use. Lord wrote that this provision reflected a concern by Congress that local residents be disturbed as little as possible and was consistent with protecting the area's wilderness qualities. The judge noted that section 5 (b) was included to prevent the uprooting of people and provide a "smooth transition for local residents to the new management plan of the BWCAW."[28] He rejected the argument that the fifteen lakes included in the forced buyout provision were arbitrarily chosen by Congress. Lord stated they were chosen because they would be most affected by the new motor restrictions.

The plaintiffs also challenged section 5 (c) of the statute. It stated that resort owners on certain lakes could force the federal government to buy their property. This decision by private citizens to sell their property, however, required other owners on the lake to give the government the right to buy them out. The Alliance and other parties in the suit alleged that Congress had no right to delegate this power to private citizens. In rejecting this argument, Lord held that federal legislators had no intention when deciding management policy for the Boundary Waters to delegate such authority.[29] He noted that the federal government had an interest in a lake when it bought a parcel of land along its shore. It thus had the right of first refusal to buy other property along the shores of the lakes specified in the statute.

Lord ruled that Congress had acted within its power by banning motors as a means to realize its goal of preserving the wilderness qualities of the canoe area. He noted, "There was sufficient testimony before the Congress for it to conclude that the whine or roar of motors within a wilderness destroys solitude."[30] The judge held that individuals who believed their property rights were violated could bring a specific case and state a claim for relief. No such claims were made in *NAPO v. U.S.,* and Lord declined to rule on whether section 5 had the effect of the taking of private property without fair compensation.

Minnesota v. Bergland challenged the authority of Congress to regulate the water surface area of the border lakes wilderness. Lord noted that Congress, through the property clause in Article IV of the Constitution, had the right to regulate the use of property that was not owned by the federal government. He cited *U.S. v. Brown,* a case that recognized the authority of Congress to regulate nonfederal property when failure to do so would frustrate the intent of a federal statute. Carl Brown, while using a boat to hunt ducks on waters in Voyageurs National Park, had been fined by federal officials. Brown's use of a firearm had been in violation of regulations for managing the park, and the court held that his actions "constituted a significant interference with the prescribed uses of the public park." Brown's attorney had argued that the regulation was not enforceable on water bodies inside the park because the state exercised jurisdiction over them. In a similar way of reasoning, Lord stated, "Congress had determined that regulation of motorized uses on lands and waters within the boundaries of the BWCAW is a needful prescription respecting the wilderness."[31] The only limitation on the power of Congress to regulate nonfederal property was that its decisions be reasonable. The judge found that the decision by Congress to reduce the water surface available for motor use was a rational outcome of its intent to preserve the wilderness qualities of the Boundary Waters.

Lord noted that section 16 (a) of the 1978 statute provided for shared jurisdiction of the state and federal governments in managing the area. This section did not set aside the state's right to control water surface use but only prevented the state from allowing motorized travel on lakes where such travel was banned by federal law. Lord argued that the 1978 act did, however, allow Minnesota to impose stricter regulations on motorized travel than those mandated by Congress. The judge pointed out that the state could use its authority to prevent mining in the Boundary Waters by restricting all motor travel across water.

In the third case, *NAPO v. Bergland,* the plaintiffs alleged that the secretary of agriculture was required by law to prepare an environmental impact statement before implementing P.L. 95-495. Lord ruled that this interpretation of section 102 (2)(c) of the National Environmental Policy Act of 1969 (NEPA) was incorrect. The administration of the 1978 statute was not, in the sense of the NEPA, a major federal action.[32] Congress had directed the secretary of agriculture to implement the law, and as an executive official, he did not have the authority to act against the intent of Congress. In his lengthy opinion, Lord claimed that his decision on the three cases was a victory for all parties in the dispute. The ruling upheld provisions in P.L. 95-495 to restrict motor use but also recognized state jurisdiction over waters in the canoe area.

The Decision Appealed. The Ely-Winton Alliance, in an issue of its newsletter, claimed that Lord's opinion had been written "in accordance with legislative rhetoric."[33] The group claimed that his decision used many of the same arguments employed by the wilderness interests to get the BWCA Wilderness Act of 1978 passed. The group opposed the court's use of the property clause, arguing that the decision made it appear as if there were not "an acre of land or waters anywhere in the U.S. that the Feds can't regulate." The newsletter argued that Lord had ignored a decline in area property values and the overall negative economic results of the new law. The newsletter stated: "We must all work together if we are going to turn the tide from extreme land policies, which are taking away more and more of our freedoms by unduly restricting usage of vast reaches of American lands, as dictated by the elitist environmental cults."[34]

The Friends of the Boundary Waters Wilderness, along with other environmental groups, was pleased with the federal court's decision. Its members were disappointed, however, by the state's decision to appeal the case. Charles Dayton and Richard Rapson, two attorneys who supported the 1978 statute, argued there were three reasons why Minnesota should not appeal the decision. First, Lord's decision would be hard to overturn because it rested on sound legal reasoning.[35] Second, an appeal might jeopardize the court's favorable ruling on the state's water rights. Third, the lawyers argued, an appeal would serve only to prolong the conflict and delay efforts to secure "adequate federal financial support for the Act's implementation."

On 1 October 1980 the state filed a brief with the U.S. Circuit Court of Appeals for the Eighth District to contest the *Minnesota v. Bergland* decision. The plaintiffs in the other two cases also appealed Lord's decision, and all three were heard as *Minnesota v. Block.* On 30 September 1981 the circuit court affirmed the lower court's decision. It agreed with Lord's use of the property clause, giving Congress the power to restrict motor use in the wilderness area. The justices cited *Kleppe v. New Mexico,* a case in which the Supreme Court had attached broad powers to the property clause. In *Kleppe v. New Mexico,* the court had ruled that wild horses in the western states belonged to the federal government; it held that the property clause gave Congress authority to control the use of wild horses even when they strayed from federal onto private lands.[36] The circuit court opinion noted that Congress had passed a law in 1976 that protected wild horses and burros from being harassed and destroyed. The court ruled that this legislative protection applied to adjacent private property as well as on public lands. The decision stated, "Congress clearly has the power to dedicate federal lands for particular purposes. As a necessary incident to that power, Congress must have the ability to insure that these lands be protected against interference with their intended purpose."[37]

The state of Minnesota, along with eleven other state governments, again appealed the decision. On 8 March 1982 the U.S. Supreme Court declined to hear the case, thus eliminating the last challenge to the constitutionality of the statute. Alexander, the commissioner of the Minnesota Department of Natural Resources, reacted sarcastically to the decision, suggesting that the state could fight back by imposing certain restrictions on travel in the wilderness. For example, he suggested, aluminum canoes might be banned because they "are a product of technology and because they allow easier access to the BWCA."[38] Alexander held to his view that bans on motorized recreation by the federal government violated the state's rights.

Federal Appropriations. The 1978 act authorized the appropriation of funds to implement the various parts of the statute. These included appropriations to help resorters and outfitters located on the edge of the wilderness adjust to reductions in motorized recreation. Congress directed the Forest Service to increase motor travel in other areas of the Superior National Forest. One way to do this was to construct snowmobile trails outside the wilderness area. The statute also provided for the buying-out of resort owners who wanted to sell their property as a result of business losses.

Although P.L. 95-495 authorized the appropriation of money from the federal treasury, the funding was not automatic. Many residents in the Arrowhead Region expressed anger when Congress did not move quickly in the new session to provide the full level of funds authorized to assist the area. A Duluth newspaper noted that although funding ceilings had been specified in the legislation, the Minnesota legislators were being forced to ask for the money that Congress had promised the region. The editorial stated, "If Congress had no intention of delivering these funds, the BWCA law can only be described, for lack of better words, as legislative rape."[39] In a letter to the editor, Bruce Vento, the U.S. representative from the Fourth District in Minnesota, pointed out that authorizing and appropriating money were two separate actions. He noted that the efforts by the Minnesota delegation to get appropriations were a normal part of the legislative process.[40]

Congress did pass appropriations bills to implement P.L. 95-495 but not at the level of funding that some people claimed was needed to fully implement the law. Federal assistance was limited to the owners of edge firms, whose business depended directly on clients who visited the wilderness. The Forest Service, which administered these programs, refused to provide funds to other businesses. These groups argued, however, that their economic fortunes were affected by the altered motor rules. Those who ran motels, restaurants, food stores, gas stations, and other enterprises claimed they also needed aid. Representative Oberstar argued that financial help to communities was being misdirected, and he declared that "we have an obligation to help business depressed by the new BWCA law."[41]

The Ely Chamber of Commerce asked the Forest Service for federal assistance in developing advertisements for magazines and newspapers to sell the canoe area to a larger public. It also wanted to use the media to clarify the "misunderstandings surrounding the status of the BWCA."[42] Some local residents attributed the decline in visitor use of the border lakes wilderness in 1979 to public confusion about what uses were allowed after the new law was passed. The Chamber argued that an advertising campaign would help to bring about an increase in tourist business for everyone in the community, not just for the edge firms.

The Forest Service decided to release sixty thousand dollars for advertisements to promote wilderness recreation in the canoe area. The Ely Chamber of Commerce combined this federal funding with a grant of eighty-five thousand dollars from the Upper Great Lakes Regional Commission to "offset tourism declines in northeastern Minnesota." A spokesman for the chamber stated that some of the money would be used to convince those who wanted to vacation in the area that locals were "not an angry, fistshaking lot, an impression . . . left in the aftermath of the bitter BWCA fight."[43] He explained the rationale for the promotion funds in the following manner: " . . . if we can get attention, get the public up here, we won't need any government loans or resorts bought out."[44]

Visitor statistics kept for the canoe wilderness by the Forest Service showed a decline from 1978 to 1979 in the number of permits issued. Some agency employees pointed out that the decline in visitors might best be explained by new counting procedures. During the 1979 summer season, the Forest Service began using a single annual permit for area homeowners and resort clients who used the canoe wilderness. In 1978 these people had been counted as visitors each time they traveled in the Boundary Waters; in 1979, under the new permit system, the same users were counted only once for the entire season.[45] Many tourist-based enterprises reported a decline in earnings for the 1979 season. Robert Rehfeld, the supervisor of the Superior National Forest, noted several factors to explain why there were fewer visitors to the canoe area. These included a late spring, which left lakes still frozen in May, a national gas shortage, and a high rate of inflation. Given these factors, he argued, the specific effect of P.L. 95-495 on the decline in economic activity was difficult to measure.[46]

The Tourist Assessment Study. In May 1980 the Agricultural Extension Service, at the University of Minnesota, released a study on the needs of firms located on the edge of the Boundary Waters. The study was done to help implement section 19 of the 1978 act, which provided for "programs of financial, technical, and educational assistance to be administered to private firms and communities in the area."[47] Research for the study, which was funded by the Forest Service, was carried out in the fall of 1979. Based on an analysis of gross business sales between 1973 to 1979, the study found that edge firms were in "a state of stagnation." It stated, "Uncertainty among firm operators regarding future restrictions plus market confusion regarding present and future restrictions appear as major causes of this stagnation."[48]

The study, however, found a high potential for attracting tourist dollars to the canoe area. The researchers noted that many residents planned to expand their business operations and that "a ready national market exists for the recreational vacation experiences available through the BWCAW edge firms."[49] The study suggested that the demand for recreation could be increased by marketing the region's image as a "unique northwoods and water wilderness." It recommended preserving the border lakes in a natural state, as its primary economic value lay in its wilderness qualities. The study also noted that federal and state agencies should work to clarify policies for recreational use of the canoe area. Uncertainty about the policies following the legislative war between the two factions was partly responsible for the economic stagnation.

The study listed four things that contributed to the decline in recreation visits in 1979: a national energy shortage, high inflation levels, the BWCA Wilderness Act of 1978, and the visitor permit system.[50] The gasoline shortage and a decline in the value of the dollar made potential visitors reluctant to plan a vacation. Years of bitter debate over how the area should be used had formed a "negative image" in the minds of many potential visitors. The agency's visitor permit system played a role in the decline in that it limited access in order to protect the carrying capacity of the wilderness. The authors of the study stated, "On the one hand it presents a bureaucratic-psychological barrier; on the other, it helps to assure the quality of the experience."[51]

The study emphasized that the canoe area possessed a high potential for attracting tourists from throughout the nation. It cited a trend in the growth of outdoor recreation in national forests, which included a higher demand for low-density and undeveloped use without motors. The public wanted recreation oriented toward conserving rather than consuming resources, such as hiking and canoeing.[52] The study concluded that the canoe wilderness and surrounding lands had the qualities that could attract increased use.

The Plan for Implementation. Section 20 of the 1978 act required the Forest Service to prepare a management plan to implement the act's provisions. On 30 July 1981 the agency released a draft of its *Plan to Implement the BWCA Wilderness Act* and distributed it to individuals and groups with an interest in management of the area. The agency proposed to limit the number of visitor permits for the summer season from 85 to 67 percent of the campsite capacity in the canoe wilderness. Some objected to this plan, although the Forest Service argued it was necessary to prevent overuse of the area. The agency completed the final plan in October 1981, and it was sent to Congress by the Forest Service chief. A Duluth newspaper observed that this proposal "quite simply seems to indicate that an ever-smaller number of Americans, whose taxes support the BWCA, will have an opportunity to enjoy our public wilderness."[53]

The new restrictions banned the use of towboats with engines over twenty-five horsepower to carry canoe parties in the wilderness.[54] These restrictions, along with bans on three snowmobile routes in the canoe area, were to take effect in January 1984. The plan allowed special-use permits for snowmobiles to groom cross-country ski trails in the wilderness. This helped firms located on the edge of the wilderness to attract visitors during the winter months. The new management rules allowed motorboats access to the area at certain entry points but not at others.

The plan authorized the use of motorized equipment in the canoe wilderness for administrative purposes, including the fighting of wildfires, although the use of bulldozers to build fire lines had to be approved by the regional forester in Milwaukee.[55] Use of fire retardant drops would be approved where, if a fire were not suppressed, great damage could result. As a matter of stated policy, the agency was to rely whenever possible on natural barriers such as lakes and streams to stop fires, even if that meant losing more acreage. Two long-time residents of the canoe area, Dorothy Molter and Ben Ambrose, were also allowed to use motorized vehicles to travel to and from their cabins.

Forest Service recreation plans involved classifying the canoe wilderness into a Recreation Opportunity Spectrum: primitive, semi-primitive nonmotorized, and semiprimitive motorized.[56] The first area included the most remote parts of the area, where no motors or developed campsites would be allowed. In the second area, the agency permitted the building of campsite facilities but did not allow mechanized travel to and from them. The third type of area was the least attractive from the standpoint of wilderness purists; fixed campsites and motor use were allowed there. The agency believed that concrete fire grates and toilet units at designated campsites were "important resource protection facilities."[57]

Summary. The controversy over the property rights of private citizens who owned land adjacent to the wilderness area involved the ability to use or sell it as they chose. In the 1978 Vermilion Lake incident, some property owners feared that their lands would be threatened by new zoning rules that would restrict land uses or allow for the condemnation and buying-out of the lands. This perceived threat sent a shiver through many area residents, as they feared that the government might ban motor travel, making access to their summer homes difficult at best. The national recreation area provision in some earlier BWCA proposals also created concern among land owners along the Fernberg, Gunflint, and Echo road corridors. Many viewed this as an attempt by the federal government to zone land it did not hold title to, which limited the right of citizens to use their property as they chose. Other residents asserted that statutory restrictions imposed on the sale of private property, such as the government's right of first refusal, was unconstitutional.

Another legal issue involved Minnesota's jurisdiction over the use of water surface areas in the Boundary Waters wilderness. The state alleged that the federal government did not possess the constitutional authority to designate restrictions on motor use in the canoe area; if these restrictions were to be applied, it was a decision for the state of Minnesota to make. Until the debate began in 1975 on new legislation for managing the canoe area, the Forest Service assumed it could regulate only motorized vehicles that crossed lands owned by the federal government. The agency claimed no legal authority to regulate motors on waters in the wilderness area unless the state agreed to such authority.[58] Governor Quie viewed the court ruling that the state shared jurisdiction with the federal government as an effective loss of Minnesota's water rights. According to Judge Lord's decision, the state still retained its water rights; it could further restrict water use but could not raise motor levels above those imposed by Congress.

Residents who had an economic interest in the canoe wilderness had various attitudes about the recreation issue. Some residents agreed that it was necessary to limit visitor access in order to protect the BWCA from physical and biological damage. They supported a management policy that protected the area from excessive use.[59] Others objected to increased restrictions on the use of motors and wished to maintain mechanized travel at levels established in the Freeman directives of 1965. Established levels were acceptable, they argued, because limited motor use did not disrupt ecosystems. A few local people wanted to increase the number of motorboats and snowmobiles in the area. Wishing to increase tourism, they argued that the federal government should act to improve the region's business climate.

Opponents of motorized travel claimed that the elimination of motors would enhance the reputation of the area and make it a long-term economic asset for area communities. The best use of the area, they believed, lay in marketing it as a unique water wilderness experience. In general, the overall health of the region's economy does not appear to have been harmed by implementing P.L. 95-495. It is difficult to relate the health of the Ely and Grand Marais economies directly to implementing the 1978 BWCA Wilderness Act. There are other factors that influence economic trends, such as unemployment caused by a depressed mining industry. Several firms, however, have argued that the statute has cost them business and generally slowed economic activity in communities near the BWCA Wilderness.[60]

Two issues that continued to simmer in the Arrowhead Region after 1978 involved popular control of the area and social equity. There was a fear of government decisions made by appointed officials unresponsive to citizen demands and a concern that the federal legislative process did not truly represent the interests of northeastern Minnesotans. Many local people who supported multiple-use policies for the border lakes argued that the federal government should minimize the extent of its rules governing the canoe area. Opposed to what they viewed as federal intrusion into local affairs, they believed that decisions on management of the area should be made to promote local interests first.

Some people who lived near the Boundary Waters claimed that policy decisions on snowmobile and motorboat use had in effect been made before there was input from the local public. This had happened, they alleged, in the cases of the Selke Committee report in 1964, the Freeman directives in 1965, the Duluth snowmobile hearings in 1976, and the BWCA Wilderness Act in 1978. Opponents of these actions charged that federal officials consistently failed to take into account the impact of their policy decisions on people who lived in the area. They maintained that the legislative process that resulted in P.L. 95-495 sanctioned a decision that had already been made by those in the inner circles of power. Most observers, however, credit the Alliance with blocking a bill that would have made no concessions to multiple-use interests.

Many Alliance members accused environmentalists of being elitists. They argued that opponents of motorized recreation, through their political connections, were able to manipulate the federal government. They saw environmentalists as a well-heeled minority group organized to challenge the values of private enterprise, property rights, and the use of natural resources. This minority control of the political system, they alleged, pushed out the public. The Friends, however, argued that most visitors to the BWCA wished to travel without motors and were irritated by their presence. The Friends argued that further reductions in motorized recreation in fact reflected the popular will.

Both sides raised the question of social equity involved in the costs and benefits of motorized recreation. Those preferring to use motors argued they were being unfairly required to bear the costs associated with tighter restrictions. They claimed that the 1978 decision to further curtail motors unfairly dismissed the quid pro quo in section 4 (d)(5) of the Wilderness Act of 1964. Many environmentalists claimed it was unfair not to set aside the entire BWCA as a wilderness for use only by those who wanted to travel by nonmotorized means. The rest of the Superior National Forest was available for motorized recreation, and some visitors argued that they were still forced to compete with motorboats during trips into parts of the canoe wilderness.

Many residents strongly objected to motor bans because they curtailed their right to use the area for short excursions to fish and picnic. The residents were forced to adjust to new restrictions so that visitors who lived outside the region could avoid encounters with motors. The attachment felt by local people to the canoe area gave them a sense that in some manner the area belonged to them. This attachment to the wilderness area was matched by equally emotional responses from recreationists who, while living outside the region, also saw it as their own special area. As yearly visitors, many canoeists knew the area's landscape in a quite personal way.[61] Their emotional attachment to the canoe area also helped make the policy issue quite difficult.

7 ❧ Changing Environmental Values

Introduction. This study assumes that different beliefs, attitudes, and values determined the preferences of the two groups that used the border lakes wilderness. One group of visitors preferred to use outboard motors and snowmobiles, and the other wanted to use paddle canoes and Nordic skis. These differences in recreational tastes led to the conflict for two reasons. First, the area in question was public land owned by the federal government. Second, visitors who preferred nonmotor use were irritated by the presence of motors and wished to ban their use.

Those who opposed motorized recreation argued that this form of travel was incompatible with wilderness values. The evidence suggested that the area's biophysical properties were not damaged by limited motor use, but opponents claimed such use diminished their wilderness experience. For them, the subjective qualities of solitude and naturalness were disturbed by encounters with motorized equipment; they argued that motor use was foreign to the concept of wilderness. They entered the political arena to modify policies for managing the Boundary Waters.

Those who supported motorized recreation wanted to protect their economic interests and their right to continue established patterns of use. The conflict involved a clear difference in recreational tastes between motor and nonmotor users. A majority of local interests appeared to favor travel by motor, or at least the right to choose that form of travel. Most of the visitors who lived outside the Arrowhead Region, however, preferred to use canoes and Nordic skis. Many area residents perceived the conflict over motor use as a matter of local autonomy versus interference by outsiders. They saw established recreation uses under sudden attack by environmental groups that worked to manipulate public policy for their own selfish ends.

The people who became active in the political dispute over what form of recreation was appropriate for the area often articulated general and rather abstract ideas about what uses society should make of the natural environment. Debate over wilderness policy often centers on a concern for how human actions affect the ecosystems of natural areas. In the case of the canoe area, however, the critical policy issue was the psychological aspect of wilderness as an experience. Each side expressed different tastes, beliefs, and attitudes; each sought to settle the issue in a law that protected its values.

Although often implied rather than stated, the arguments on both sides of the recreation issue rested on philosophical differences. Because of these differences, the problem was not amenable to political compromise. In general, the forces wanting to ban travel by motors expressed biocentric ideas, while those who wished to protect existing use developed anthropocentric concepts to defend their policy choice. That is, one side argued from a life-centered view, while the other articulated a human-centered view of things. According to the first perspective, human beings should generally adapt themselves to natural constraints imposed by the environment. According to the second, humans should readily adapt nature to their purposes through the use of new technology.

Recreational Tastes. Visitors who used motors seemed more willing to allow other resource uses that nonmotor users considered incompatible with wilderness. For example, Alliance members supported continued logging in the area and relinquished this position only when alternative timber supplies outside the canoe wilderness were found. The desire by many residents not to close off options for mining and logging in the canoe area makes sense; these industries, along with tourism, form the economic base of their communities. It is one thing to be against logging if a person makes a living as a logger and another if his or her income is derived from some other source in an urban area.

Those who did not choose to travel in the canoe area with motors had their own definition of what constituted a wilderness experience. Encounters with motor users lessened the quality of the experience for nonmotor users, such as paddle canoeists and Nordic skiers. The disagreement was not over the question of whether one type of travel was somehow better or more virtuous than the other. The two sides, however, did have widely different attitudes on land use and distinct, if only implicit, values concerning how human beings should relate to the natural world.

With the introduction in 1975 of Fraser's bill for a total wilderness, the primary issue was whether canoeists should have the entire BWCA—where any form of motorized recreation was prohibited by federal law—reserved exclusively for their use. In a larger geographical context, multiple use meant that mechanized travel should not be allowed in each and every part of the Superior National Forest. Some areas should be reserved for that part of the public that preferred to visit a motor-free area. The critical question was thus whether the entire BWCA should be set aside by the government in which only nonmechanized travel was allowed. In this concept of multiple use, nonmotorized recreation may be seen as one form of use among several types. Even though travel by nonmotorized means may seem odd to some people, it is nevertheless a means preferred by others.

Aldo Leopold, who advocated a new land ethic, argued that wilderness areas "are first of all a series of sanctuaries for the primitive arts of wilderness travel, especially canoeing and packing."[1] He noted that "we who seek wilderness travel for sport are foiled when we are forced to compete with mechanized substitutes." Garrett Hardin, in an article about managing public lands, asserted that "no one should be able to enter a wilderness by mechanical means."[2] He maintained that the wilderness experience involves traveling into a natural area as well as being in it: "If we were dropped down from a line by helicopter into the middle of this experience we would miss an important part of the total experience, namely the experience of getting there." He declared, "Just unmechanized man and nature—this is a necessary ingredient of the prescription for the wilderness experience."

In a similar vein, Arthur Carhart stated, "The canoeist soaking in the spirit of the lake country at a camp in the Quetico-Superior feels cheated when an amphibian plane sets down in the next bay, fishermen pile out, get their limit, and wing away before sundown."[3] The man who first studied the BWCA for its recreation potential asserted, "With smashing suddenness we face the question of whether or not power-driven types of transportation shall convert the little remaining back country to the level of millions of acres already available for motorized travel." Carhart felt strongly about the issue, and he wanted to introduce zoning to limit motorized recreation on public lands.

Referring to recreationists who used jeeps on federal lands, Carhart claimed they should not be allowed to "run wild through back country, merely because they are able to do so."[4] New and improved forms of technology provided visitors easier access to wild areas, which before were only open to those traveling on foot, horse, or by boat. He viewed such unrestricted behavior, however, as infringing on the "rights and privileges" of others who preferred to meet the land on its own terms. He noted, "There is certainty that some jeepers will take the attitude that if they can ram their vehicles into these areas they are entitled to do so. It's their national forest, isn't it, much as anybody's?" Carhart drew an analogy between natural areas managed by the federal government and baseball fields in municipal parks. While both were owned by the public, he argued, the jeep operator would not expect to drive his vehicle across the baseball diamond. Carhart claimed that in this case the jeep operator "would properly recognize its allocation to another recreational use." He argued that resolving the public lands issue of motor use required a "zoning of outdoor areas to protect recreation values."

From the perspective of pro-motor advocates who lived in the region, however, it appeared that outside forces were eliminating their preferred use in a most unfair way. To satisfy their concept of a pristine wilderness experience, people who opposed motors were willing to ignore the interests and preferences of local people. The Alliance applied the idea of multiple use only to the million-acre BWCA, and not to other blocks of public land in northeastern Minnesota. Many local people believed that the canoe area should continue to be used for both forms of recreation, as well as for logging.

It should be remembered that although motor-free zones have a

place on federal lands, the Boundary Waters presents a peculiar problem. On the one hand, it is excellent terrain for extended canoe camping trips. On the other, there is a clear history of motor use in the
area, and in this sense a tradition of public use has been firmly established. To ignore this historical reality is to court the ill will of local
people. Many residents might agree in theory that motor-free zones
are justified on some federal lands, but they do not want such a policy
where they live.

Some residents who supported motorized travel in the area argued that the basic issue was the right of individuals to choose how to
enjoy their leisure time. John Chelesnik, an Ely resident, opposed
efforts by environmentalists to ban motors in the Boundary Waters:

> We're not advocating one use over another, the way the wilder-
> ness people are, but multiple use. It's a human rights issue, and
> we don't want to exclude anyone. There's plenty of room for
> cross-country skiing and canoeing and plenty of room for snow-
> mobiles and motorboats. People want to close off the woods and
> lakes so you can't use them, all for some philosophic ideal, and
> that's stupid."[5]

Chelesnik rejected the purist standard of the antimotor interests, but
his position ignored the fact that those interests were driven away
from the area by the noise of motors.[6] His statement showed a complete unawareness of the other side of the issue. First, environmentalists didn't want to close off the area from use, only to make it a
motor-free zone where visitors would not be able to travel with mechanized assistance. Second, the wilderness experience as a philosophical ideal was cherished by many antimotor people, and they were
willing to defend that ideal in the political arena.

Representative Oberstar did not ridicule the desire for a motor-
free area in the canoe area. He accepted it as a legitimate desire and
proposed dividing the one-million acre area into two parts, one of
which allowed only travel without motors. Oberstar's 1975 BWCA
bill can be seen as an attempt to protect some level of motor use in the
area by offering a compromise. He knew that political trends on the
national level favored antimotor interests and that retaining established motorized recreation use was unlikely. Given his preference,
Oberstar would probably have also liked to maintain the existing
management framework, but he saw this as a politically unfeasible
goal.

It is again important not to overlook the history of motorized recreation in the border lakes area. Many local people pointed out that they were being displaced and that a prior tradition of use was being conveniently ignored. They became very agitated when environmental issues were confused with recreational tastes. Some Alliance members argued that the Friends willfully misrepresented the issue of ecological damage, giving the impression to the general public that unless motors were banned the area would be destroyed. There was, however, an environmental issue involved in the aesthetic values that antimotor partisans sought to protect. While it was true that limited motor use did not damage the area's physical or biological environment, it did detract from the psychological atmosphere sought by a certain type of visitor. To understand this thinking, one must return to the concept of wilderness as a state of mind.

People who visit a federal wilderness area enter it in search of a special outdoor experience. The wilderness experience involves a mental state that varies from individual to individual. As a consequence of the subjective nature of the experience, each individual has a different concept of what wilderness is. For one person, the pure naturalness and solitude of a remote drainage in the Brooks Range of northern Alaska is the standard by which to measure true wilderness. For another, "a drive down the Blue Ridge Parkway in Virginia may be as much wilderness as he will ever see. Or ever want to."[7] The mental state of a wilderness visitor is determined to some extent by the environmental conditions that surround him or her. But the attitudes that a visitor brings into a natural area play a significant part in how he or she interprets the quality of an outdoor experience.

The concept of wilderness has been debated for years, and there is still not complete agreement on what it is or how to measure it; it is subject to different interpretations over time as cultural values evolve. For example, Sigurd Olson argued that the physical size of a natural area isn't the crucial element for a true communion with wilderness. He claimed that wilderness can be experienced as well in "a small patch of tundra with its mosses, lichens, and grasses as from a great stand of primeval forest."[8] Both areas are able to transmit the story of natural evolution to the careful observer. Olson noted, however, that while a few square feet may provide a sense of wild nature, a larger area must be preserved to protect complete ecosystems.

Roderick Nash pointed out that different cultures have different perceptions of wilderness. He argued that the Japanese, in contrast to Americans, "have long approached the problem of communion with nature with a different set of cultural assumptions."[9] Nash noted "the superior ability of the Japanese to derive pleasure and meaning from nature." He emphasized that the Japanese sense of the natural world comes from the beholder's perspective:

> it depends on placing oneself in the proper frame of mind, not on entering a particular environment. . . . It follows then, that the huge, wild reserves are irrelevant to the Japanese quest. The Japanese can see in a single leaf what, for an American, would require a sequoia if not a park full of them. This is why the formal garden is so important in the Japanese tradition of nature appreciation. Here, in miniature, in metaphor, the whole is represented.[10]

Wilderness Values and Paradigm Shifts. The concept of a paradigm shift has been used by social scientists who study the attitudes, values, and beliefs that modern humans have about the natural world.[11] They argue that industrialized democracies are undergoing a transition in cultural values toward a new way of seeing the environment. This value shift is a result of a growing awareness in technically advanced societies that the planet has ecological limits. The expansion of the human population and the attendant increased rate of resource consumption is depleting and disrupting nature and continues to do so. Depletion results in fewer natural resources available for human use, and disruption results in damage to ecological processes and life support systems. The growing awareness of the scarcity of resources has stimulated the search for new ways to relate to the natural world.[12]

The old cultural paradigm or world view that has shaped American attitudes and behavior toward the natural environment is perhaps nowhere more clearly set down than in the political writings of John Locke. In his concept of property this English philosopher posits a strict separation between human beings and the natural world.[13] Locke's is one of the most concise statements of an individualist and materialist approach to the environment that has been written. Locke argues that the natural world, and all biological and physical resources found therein, exist for the exclusive use of people. The environment is worthless except insofar as it provides for human needs and wants, and he views wilderness as a waste of resources. The human species, he argues, has been able to vastly increase its population and material conditions through applying reason and industry to reshape the natural world.

This material achievement has created a problem in that twentieth century humans appear to be moving beyond the capacity of the environment to sustain the demands of modern civilization. Paradoxically, the species' success in controlling nature has also been its failure. This seeming contradiction helps to explain the rise of environmentalism as a political movement and a set of ideas, values, and beliefs. The goal of environmentalism is to restructure how humans think about and behave toward the natural world by making public policies that promote environmental quality. Such policies require humans in many cases to adapt to natural forces, processes, and conditions instead of dominating the environment through sheer technical ability.

William Catton and Riley Dunlap have outlined some emerging attitudes toward nature that they refer to as a New Ecological Paradigm.[14] They distinguish this view of the world from the traditional values, which they call the Human Exemptionalist Paradigm. In the exemptionalist view, man is not a part of the natural environment. Anthropocentric man views himself as exempt from the physical and biological laws that govern the ecological balance of the planet. Man has stepped outside nature and views himself as securely located within the artificial world he has constructed. Humans exist on a different order of being than the rest of nature by virtue of their ability to reason and their technical accomplishments. But biocentric thinkers, who are exponents of the New Ecological Paradigm, believe that science confirms the close dependence of human beings on the natural order of things and that man must adapt his collective behavior to fit within the ecological limits of the world.

Catton and Dunlap discuss four assumptions that characterize the Human Exemptionalist Paradigm.[15] The first assumption is that human beings are distinct from all other forms of life on the planet. The second assumption is that all events in the world that matter to man are the result of purposive human actions. That is, man is the exclusive maker of his world by virtue of his intellect, and through the use of logic and will he can do whatever he wants. The third assumption is that man exists in a world that provides him with limitless opportunities; there are no boundaries imposed by the natural environment on human desires and actions. The fourth assumption is that human history is progressive; that is, the future will bring ever better conditions for man.

Catton and Dunlap contrast the exemptionalist view of how humans should relate to the natural environment with the New Ecological Paradigm. The emerging biocentric world view assumes that humans are but one of many life forms that exist on the planet. A second assumption of this social theory is that natural forces exert a great effect on the way that people live and that in many respects these forces cannot be controlled by human actions. The third assumption of the ecological paradigm is that there are clear and unavoidable limits placed by nature on what people can do. The resources of the planet are limited, and its life-support systems are vulnerable to human disruption. Lastly, the New Ecological Paradigm assumes that people cannot use advances in science and technology to move beyond the basic limits imposed by nature on human actions.

These contrasting views of how humans and nature relate are simplifications of extremely complex social realities. These paradigms of basic cultural values can only state in imprecise ways the hypothetical transition in human perceptions toward a biocentric perspective. This is so largely because cultural values, especially when they are in a transition state, are mostly unspoken and implicit. Only when major collisions of two sets of social values occur is it possible to attempt an analysis of them. The concept of a paradigm shift facilitates such a study because it provides a larger framework in which to look at opposing views toward the natural world. The 1978 decision by Congress to decrease the level of motorized recreation in the BWCA Wilderness may be seen as one policy example of a shift in national values toward the environment.

The first assumption of the two paradigms described by Catton and Dunlap focus on whether man views himself as distinct from the natural environment, or as an intrinsic component along with other plant and animal species. According to the biocentric perspective, man is but one of many forms of life that inhabit the earth. The visitor to the wilderness area who uses motorized means of travel has more equipment between himself and the lake environment than the visitor who uses his own physical power. The separation of man from nature by mechanized equipment makes the visitor less a part of his surroundings. This is not to imply that nonmotorized travel is better than motorized travel. Man is, however, more dependent on nature and closer to the condition in which other life forms exist while traveling in a canoe or on skis. Visitors who use motors, therefore, accommodate nature to themselves, rather than accommodating themselves to nature. With fewer artifacts interposed between humans and nature, the wilderness experience is more direct and results in a heightened appreciation of nature. The visitor moves across the landscape at a slower pace than is the case in a motorboat or snowmobile. This reduced speed allows a closer observation of the natural world, including the way things sound in a wild area when there are no artificial noises.

A second assumption of the two paradigms posited by Catton and Dunlap centers on whether people view their civilized world as shaped more by human actions or natural causes. The view of the biocentrist is that the laws of nature continue to play a critical role in shaping the world of roads, farms, factories, and cities that humans have made. Less equipment and more direct contact with nature sets the stage for a greater awareness of the dependence of humans on the environment for their survival. Within the solitude of a wilderness area, people find themselves in a world where they are visitors with little control over natural processes. Such an experience imparts to individuals a sense of their place in nature and an appreciation of the complexity of a wilderness environment unmodified by human actions. One can view the human experience as part of an ecological mosaic within which he both acts and is acted upon by forces often beyond his ability to control.

The third assumption involves the degree to which humans believe that nature places constraints on their behavior. The biocentric advocate contends that there are inherent limits on human actions that are imposed by the biology of the species and the natural laws that govern ecosystems. Man needs to restrain his behavior toward the rest of the natural world so that he does not overshoot the carrying capacity of the planet.[16] Visitors who travel by land and water using their own physical effort gain a clearer sense of the constraints imposed by nature on human actions. The use of motorized equipment for wilderness travel greatly extends the distance people can cover in a single day. Those who limit themselves to hiking or using paddle canoes, snowshoes, or Nordic skis cannot traverse nearly the amount of area. Humans possess the capacity through technology to establish motor routes in any part of the canoe wilderness they desire. But such economic development is not permitted as a matter of public policy, as most recreational users prefer to retain the area in its natural state. The visitor who travels without a motor appears more willing to work within the natural constraints imposed by the area's terrain, accepting the physical limits imposed by nature.

The last assumption discussed by Catton and Dunlap involves how humans believe material progress in advanced industrial societies is affected by natural constraints, such as limited resources. Those who support a high rate of economic development believe that human progress is without limits. If depleting resources or disrupting ecosystems creates problems for human society, science and technology can overcome the obstacles. The exemptionalist view is not shared by environmentalists, who argue that people must learn to work inside the basic ecological limits on human actions imposed by the natural world. The visitor to the BWCA who chooses not to use a motorized means of travel appears willing to forego the convenience of this form of transportation. This willingness may be viewed as a temporary suspension of the advantages that humans exert over nature through technical inventions. Those who entered the political fight to further limit motor use in the canoe wilderness believed that motors were an inappropriate form of technology. The desire to set aside certain federal lands free from economic development and mechanized access shows a growing consensus that some areas of the earth should remain in their original state. They should be free not only from human-induced changes, but also from artifacts such as motors that detract from the wilderness character of the natural area.

An anthropocentric view centers on the idea that nature should be used for human purposes, leading to further material and technical progress. According to this view, which takes a utilitarian approach to land management, natural resources exist primarily for human purposes. The biocentric view, on the other hand, takes a life-centered approach to the environment. According to it, human beings are integral members of biotic communities. The preservation of one million acres of forest and lakes in northeastern Minnesota, although it may mean the loss of some economic values, emphasizes a setting where people can appreciate nature free from the sights and sounds of motors. The elimination of mechanized travel helps to protect the primitive, tranquil character of the canoe wilderness.

If humans consider themselves a part of the natural world, they should be willing to place certain limits on their behavior in order to protect the environment. An expression of this in terms of public policy is the preservation of wilderness areas. Setting aside such areas reflects a restraint on man's part not to employ technical means to alter ecosystems for utilitarian ends. It is, as Aldo Leopold suggests, the extension of ethical values into relations between human society and the natural world.[17] This new environmental paradigm or land ethic is implicit in such federal statutes as the National Environmental Policy Act of 1969 (P.L. 91-190), among others.

Public Policy Dilemmas. Preserving wilderness from changes caused by humans can be quite difficult. The results of human actions, even from great distances away as is the case with acid rain, can greatly disrupt ecosystems.[18] Some groups want Congress to classify and manage more federal land as wilderness, restricting the use of such land to primitive recreation. Those who support resource development, however, do not want more acreage included in the national preservation system. The political history of the canoe area offers some insights into policy dilemmas associated with the management of wilderness lands.

In administering the Wilderness Act of 1964, the Forest Service has adopted a biocentric view for managing wilderness.[19] The agency maintains that only unaltered land should be classified as wilderness and managed to protect its primitive qualities. The agency's position is that while wilderness is for human use, such use must fit within the carrying capacity of the area. In other words, visitors should adjust their actions to the natural conditions imposed by wilderness areas.

Similarly, Richard Costley argues that only truly pristine federal lands should be classified legally as wilderness. Costley believes that designating lands altered by human actions will lead to problems in managing such areas. He thinks that high standards of naturalness and solitude should be maintained to preserve the quality of the national preservation system. He asserts that the purist interpretation of statutory wilderness best describes the intent of the 1964 statute. He views the designation of the BWCA as a wilderness a mistake, calling section 4 (d)(5) an "unfortunate accident":

> definitely unfortunate for the BWCA and potentially unfortunate for the Wilderness System. Undoubtedly one of the most unique and spectacular recreation areas in the National Forest System, it clearly is not wilderness in the context of the objective of the Act itself, and wishful thinking of some to the contrary, it never can be. Managed as it deserves to be it can provide a near primitive recreation experience without equal. Managed under the constrains specified for the System — as some would have it — this would be impossible and the area would be neither fish nor fowl.[20]

Another school of thought advocates modifying the natural environment so that it can better accommodate visitors. Eric Jubler, who supports this position, argues that wilderness areas should be developed so that extensive use by the public is possible.[21] To promote this vision of mass recreation, he wants to build tramways and hotel complexes in remote and rugged areas so that many more people can visit and enjoy such areas. Jubler's idea is similar to the use of the Alps by the Europeans. He thinks that scenic areas of exceptional beauty should be opened to extensive human use.

Should federal lands with a history of multiple use be included in the national preservation system? The effects of past logging, now-destroyed resorts and cabins, developed campsite units, heavily traveled portages, non-native plant and animal species, and motorized equipment all attest to the reality that the canoe area is a semi-wilderness. The region's ecosystems have undergone changes as a result of human intervention. For example, the woodland caribou, a native species, no longer inhabits the region, although there are signs that it may be migrating back into the area. The canoe area has over two thousand campsites, each of which include a concrete fire grate, box toilet, picnic table, and a cleared area for pitching tents.

Although the border lakes area has been altered in several ways by man, it is the only wilderness of its kind in the United States. There are large areas of virgin timber, and the area is dotted with lakes, rivers, streams, and portages that offer ideal conditions for canoe camping. Those who support its wilderness status contend that by eliminating incompatible uses and letting wildfires burn the region's ecology will in time return to a natural balance.

Those who oppose wilderness status for the BWCA argue its natural history is too interwoven with human uses and that government policies curtailing traditional multiple uses are unfair. The area contains timber stands of commercial value. It may also have nickel and copper deposits of economic value along the Duluth Complex. The area could be developed by constructing roads. If this area were privately owned, there probably would be a brisk real estate market. This would stimulate the local economy and increase the revenues of county governments, at least in the short run. But it would also lead to the loss of the character associated with the region's unique recreation qualities. Such a loss of wilderness character would likely impair the area's long-term economic well-being. The BWCA will likely remain a federal wilderness area, but how it is managed will probably remain in the realm of political debate.

APPENDIX 1 ◠ Chronology

1902, June. U.S. General Land Office, at request of Minnesota Forestry Commissioner Andrews, sets aside 500,000 acres in border lakes region from private acquisition.

1909, February. President Roosevelt establishes Superior National Forest.

1911, March. Congress passes Weeks Act, which gives Forest Service authority to purchase private lands for increasing national forest acreage.

1919. Carhart prepares recreation report for canoe area.

1925, September. Backus, paper mill industrialist, proposes to build series of dams to flood portions of border lakes; International Joint Commission opens hearings.

1926, September. Secretary of Agriculture Jardine establishes 640,000-acre roadless area in Superior National Forest.

1928, April. Quetico-Superior Council formed to protect wilderness lands on both sides of international border; Oberholtzer named first president.

1930, July. Congress passes Shipstead-Nolan Act, which prohibits logging within four hundred feet of shorelines and requires water surface areas to remain at present levels.

1934, April. International Joint Commission recommends against request by Backus to flood border lakes region with series of dams. *June.* President Roosevelt creates Quetico-Superior Committee to advise federal agencies on resource policy issues in region.

1939, July. Forest Service approves U-Regulations, which provides canoe area with added protection from economic development.

1941. Forest Service officials create "no-cut" Interior Zone and outer Portal Zone, where agency may permit timber sales.

1948, June. Congress passes Thye-Blatnik Act, which gives Forest Service authority to purchase private inholdings in canoe area.

1949, December. President Truman signs Executive Order 10092 banning airplanes from landing on water bodies inside three roadless areas.

1956, June. More federal funds appropriated to implement Thye-Blatnik Act; other two roadless units included as purchase areas. U.S. Senator Humphrey introduces first wilderness bill in Congress, which includes Minnesota's canoe area. *December.* Ely citi-

zen group meets with Humphrey in St. Paul; discuss changes in
bill to protect traditional multiple uses.

1957, January. Humphrey's revised wilderness bill includes section 4
(d)(5), which permits continued logging and established uses of
motorboats. *June.* Forest Service Chief McCardle testifies in
Senate hearing against wilderness bill.

1958, January. Forest Service renames three roadless units Boundary
Waters Canoe Area; extends size to near-present borders.

1960, June. Congress passes Multiple Use-Sustained Yield Act;
wilderness identified as one type of national forest land use.

1964, May. Secretary of Agriculture Freeman appoints Selke Committee to study and recommend new BWCA resource management
policies. *September.* Congress passes Wilderness Act; the act includes BWCA in national preservation system and authorizes secretary to determine specific land-use policies. *December.* Selke
Committee submits final report to secretary; recommends zoning
motorboat use and banning snowmobiles.

1965, January. Freeman's initial directive establishes nineteen motorboat routes (62 percent water area); bans snowmobiles in canoe
wilderness. *January.* Boundary Waters Resources Committee objects to secretary's decision; promotes increased levels of logging
and motor travel. *July.* Superior National Forest officials submit
revised BWCA plan, which defines snowmobiles as "winterized
watercraft" and allows on routes open to motorboats. *December.*
Freeman's final BWCA directives permit motorboats on nineteen
routes and snowmobiles on twenty-one routes.

1972. President Nixon signs Executive Order 11644, which bans
mechanized travel in federal wilderness areas.

1974, June. Superior National Forest officials submit new BWCA
management plan and EIS; propose ban on snowmobiles in 1980.
October. Dayton, Sierra Club attorney, appeals administrative
decision; requests snowmobile use be banned in spring 1975.

1975, April. Forest Service Chief McGuire decides in favor of ban.
October. U.S. Representative Oberstar introduces BWCA bill in
Congress that redesignates part of area as wilderness and other
part as national recreation area where multiple uses allowed. *No-
vember.* Forest Service Chief McGuire decides to delay enforcing
BWCA snowmobile ban one year.

1976, January. Oberstar reintroduces BWCA bill in Ninety-fifth Congress. *February.* Minntour, Nordic ski group, sues secretary of
agriculture; challenges discretion to ban snowmobiles. Secretary
of Agriculture Butz responds to uproar in Arrowhead Region;

holds Duluth hearing on BWCA snowmobile issue. *May.* Friends formed as coalition of environmental groups to lobby Congress for total wilderness bill. *June.* U.S. Representative Fraser, at Friends' request, introduces BWCA bill, which bans motors as incompatible with wilderness values. *September.* Butz upholds decision by McGuire to ban snowmobiles.

1977, January. In *Minntour v. Butz,* Judge Alsop rules secretary of agriculture has authority in Wilderness Act of 1964 to determine BWCA snowmobile use. *May.* Alliance formed as coalition of local interests in BWCA communities; promotes modified Oberstar bill to protect established multiple uses. *July.* U.S. Representative Vento holds subcommittee hearings in St. Paul and Ely on BWCA issues. *August.* House Subcommittee on Parks and Insular Affairs, chaired by Representative Burton, holds BWCA hearings in Washington, D.C.; Carter administration officials propose motor bans similar to those in Fraser bill.

1978, January. U.S. Senator Humphrey dies after prolonged illness. Mass snowmobile protest ride by multiple-use supporters into BWCA; Forest Service personnel arrest violators. *February.* Oberstar's fourth and last BWCA bill rejected by Burton's subcommittee. Burton-Vento bill (H.R. 12250) emerges from House subcommittee; compromise supported by Friends but rejected by Alliance. *March.* Wilderness boundary line misdrawn over small bay in Vermilion Lake; action generates anger and suspicion in northeastern Minnesota. *April.* Alliance leaders sponsor wild game dinner in Virginia, Minnesota; U.S. Senator Anderson supports multiple-use cause. Cook County Alliance chapter holds demonstration against Forest Service at district office in Grand Marais. Ely Alliance chapter demonstrates in Duluth to protest passage of H.R. 12250 by full House Interior Committee. *June.* H.R. 12250 passed by House in floor vote, over objections by Oberstar and Alliance. Alliance protesters demonstrate against Fraser at DFL state convention in St. Paul. Anderson introduces S. 3242 in Congress, which retains existing motorboat use and slightly reduces snowmobile travel; Alliance supports, while Friends view it as unacceptable. *August.* Members of Senate Subcommittee on Parks and Recreation visit BWCA to better understand issues. Alliance and Friends send negotiators to Washington, D.C., at request of Senator Abouresk in attempt to resolve motor-use issues. Dayton-Walls compromise, which proposes to reduce motor levels by nearly half, strongly rejected by Alliance chapters in Ely and Grand Marais. Anderson decides to incorporate Dayton-Walls compromise into H.R. 12250; Alliance argues its cause is betrayed. Alliance members in Ely set up roadblocks to BWCA to protest Anderson's new bill. *September.* Fraser defeated in primaries for DFL Senate ticket, a loss attributed by Alliance to BWCA position. *October.* H.R. 12250 with Dayton-Walls compromise passes Senate. Conference committee approves amended H.R. 12250; Senate version of bill sent back to House floor for approval. H.R. 12250 passes House vote over Oberstar's protest. Senate passes BWCA bill in last hours of Ninety-fifth Congress. President Carter signs P.L. 95-495 into law. *November.* Anderson loses Senate seat to Republican candidate.

1979, January. Ely-Winton Alliance incorporated; other chapters in northeastern Minnesota become inactive. *July.* Alliance requests injunction in U.S. District court to delay implementing P.L. 95-495; request denied. *August.* Alliance refiles lawsuit as *NAPO v. U.S.* in federal court in Duluth; alleges individual rights violated. *December.* State of Minnesota files lawsuit, *Minnesota v. Bergland,* against federal government to contest alleged violation of BWCA water rights.

1980, January. Alliance files second lawsuit, *NAPO v. Bergland;* alleges secretary of agriculture must write EIS before implementing P.L. 95-495. *May.* Agricultural Extension Service releases tourist needs study for BWCA region. *July.* U.S. District Judge Lord rules against plaintiffs on all counts in three cases. *October.* State government and Alliance file briefs with U.S. Court of Appeals for the Eighth Circuit to contest decision.

1981, July. Forest Service releases draft BWCA management plan to implement P.L. 95-495. *September.* Appeals court affirms district court decision in *Minnesota v. Block. October.* Forest Service releases final BWCA management plan after extensive public comments.

1982, March. U.S. Supreme Court refuses to hear *Minnesota v. Block.*

1984, January. Snowmobile use banned on three routes, and further reductions on motorboat use phased in.

APPENDIX 2 ✑ Public Law 95-495

Public Law 95-495
95th Congress

An Act

To designate the Boundary Waters Canoe Area Wilderness, to establish the Boundary Waters Canoe Area Mining Protection Area, and for other purposes.

Oct. 21, 1978

[H.R. 12250]

Be it enacted by the Senate and House of Representatives of the United States of America in Congress assembled,

FINDINGS

SECTION 1. The Congress finds that it is necessary and desirable to provide for the protection, enhancement, and preservation of the natural values of the lakes, waterways, and associated forested areas known (before the date of enactment of this Act) as the Boundary Waters Canoe Area, and for the orderly management of public use and enjoyment of that area as wilderness, and of certain contiguous lands and waters, while at the same time protecting the special qualities of the area as a natural forest-lakeland wilderness ecosystem of major esthetic, cultural, scientific, recreational and educational value to the Nation.

Boundary Waters
Canoe Area
Wilderness,
designation;
Boundary Waters
Canoe Area
Mining
Protection Area,
establishment.

PURPOSES

SEC. 2. It is the purpose of this Act to provide for such measures respecting the areas designated by this Act as the Boundary Waters Canoe Area Wilderness and Boundary Waters Canoe Area Mining Protection Area as will—

(1) provide for the protection and management of the fish and wildlife of the wilderness so as to enhance public enjoyment and appreciation of the unique biotic resources of the region,

(2) protect and enhance the natural values and environmental quality of the lakes, streams, shorelines and associated forest areas of the wilderness,

(3) maintain high water quality in such areas,

(4) minimize to the maximum extent possible, the environmental impacts associated with mineral development affecting such areas,

(5) prevent further road and commercial development and restore natural conditions to existing temporary roads in the wilderness, and

(6) provide for the orderly and equitable transition from motorized recreational uses to nonmotorized recreational uses on those lakes, streams, and portages in the wilderness where such mechanized uses are to be phased out under the provisions of this Act.

BOUNDARY WATERS CANOE AREA WILDERNESS DESIGNATION AND MAP

SEC. 3. The areas generally depicted as wilderness on the map entitled "Boundary Waters Canoe Area Wilderness and Boundary Waters Canoe Area Mining Protection Area" dated September 1978, comprising approximately one million and seventy-five thousand five hundred acres, are hereby designated as the Boundary Waters Canoe Area Wilderness (hereinafter referred to as the "wilderness"). Such designation shall supersede the designation of the Boundary Waters Canoe

16 USC 1132
note.

16 USC 1132.

Publication in
Federal Register.

Filing with
congressional
committees.

Area under section 3(a) of the Wilderness Act (78 Stat. 890) and such map shall supersede the map on file pursuant to such section. The map of the wilderness shall be on file and available for public inspection in the offices of the Supervisor of the Superior National Forest and of the Chief, United States Forest Service. The Secretary of Agriculture, hereinafter referred to as "The Secretary," shall, as soon as practicable but in no event later than one year after the date of enactment of this Act, publish a detailed legal description and map showing the boundaries of the wilderness in the Federal Register. Such map and description shall be filed with the Committee on Interior and Insular Affairs of the House of Representatives and the Committee on Energy and Natural Resources of the United States Senate. Such map and description shall have the same force and effect as if included in this Act. Correction of clerical and typographical errors in such legal description and map may be made.

ADMINISTRATION

Sec. 4. (a) The Secretary shall administer the wilderness under the provisions of this Act, the Act of January 3, 1975 (88 Stat. 2096; 16 U.S.C. 1132 note), the Wilderness Act of 1964 (78 Stat. 890, 16 U.S.C. 1131-1136), and in accordance with other laws, rules and regulations generally applicable to areas designated as wilderness.

Repeal.
16 USC 1133.

(b) Paragraph (5) of section 4(d) of the Wilderness Act of 1964 is hereby repealed and paragraphs (6), (7), and (8) of such section 4(d) are hereby redesignated as paragraphs (5), (6), and (7).

Motorboat use.

(c) Effective on January 1, 1979, the use of motorboats is prohibited within the wilderness designated by this Act, and that portion within the wilderness of all lakes which are partly within the wilderness, except for the following:

(1) On the following lakes, motorboats with motors of no greater than twenty-five horsepower shall be permitted: Fall, Lake County; Newton, Lake County; Moose, Lake County; Newfound, Lake County; Sucker, Lake County; Snowbank, Lake County; East Bearskin, Cook County; South Farm, Lake County; Trout, Saint Louis County; Basswood, except that portion generally north of the narrows at the north end of Jackfish Bay and north of a point on the international boundary between Ottawa Island and Washington Island; Saganaga, Cook County, except for that portion west of American Point; *Provided:* That, on the following lakes, until January 1, 1984, the horsepower limitations described in this paragraph shall not apply to towboats registered with the Secretary: Moose, Lake County; Newfound, Lake County; Sucker, Lake County; Saganaga, Cook County, as limited in this paragraph.

(2) On the following lakes and river, motorboats with motors no greater than ten horsepower shall be permitted: Clearwater, Cook County; North Fowl, Cook County; South Fowl, Cook County; Island River east of Lake Isabella, Lake County; Sea Gull, that portion generally east of Threemile Island, Cook County; Alder, Cook County; Canoe, Cook County.

(3) On the following lakes, or specified portions of lakes, motorboats with motors of no greater than ten horsepower shall be permitted until the dates specified: Basswood River to and including Crooked Lake, Saint Louis and Lake Counties, until January 1, 1984; Carp Lake, the Knife River, and Knife Lake, Lake County, until January 1, 1984; Sea Gull, Cook County, that portion generally west of Threemile Island, until January 1, 1999; Brule,

Cook County, until January 1, 1994, or until the termination of operation of any resort adjacent to Brule Lake in operation as of 1977, whichever occurs first.

(4) On the following lakes, or specified portions of lakes, motorboats with motors of no greater than twenty-five horsepower shall be permitted until January 1, 1984: Birch, Lake County; Basswood, Lake County, that portion generally north of the narrows at the north end of Jackfish Bay and north of a point on the international boundary between Ottawa Island and Washington Island.

(d) The detailed legal description and map to be published pursuant to section 3 of this Act shall contain a description of the various areas where the motorized uses permitted by this section are located. No provision of this section shall be construed to limit mechanical portages or the horsepower of motors used on motorboats in the following areas within the wilderness:

Exemptions.

Little Vermilion Lake, Saint Louis County; Loon River, Saint Louis County; Loon Lake, Saint Louis County; that portion of the Lac La Croix, Saint Louis County, south of Snow Bay and east of Wilkins Bay.

(e) For the purposes of this Act, a snowmobile is defined as any motorized vehicle which is designed to operate on snow or ice. The use of snowmobiles in the wilderness designated by this Act is not permitted except that the Secretary may permit snowmobiles, not exceeding forty inches in width, on (1) the overland portages from Crane Lake to Little Vermilion Lake in Canada, and from Sea Gull River along the eastern portion of Saganaga Lake to Canada, and (2) on the following routes until January 1, 1984:

Snowmobile use.

Vermilion Lake portage to and including Trout Lake; Moose Lake to and including Saganaga Lake via Ensign, Vera and Knife Lakes; East Bearskin Lake to and including Pine Lake via Alder Lake and Canoe Lake.

In addition to the routes listed above, the Secretary may issue special use permits for the grooming by snowmobiles of specified cross-country ski trails for day use near existing resorts.

Trail grooming, special permits.

(f) The Secretary is directed to develop and implement, as soon as practical, entry point quotas for use of motorboats within the wilderness portions of the lakes listed in subsection c, the quota levels to be based on such criteria as the size and configuration of each lake, and the amount of use on that lake: *Provided*, That the quota established for any one year shall not exceed the average actual annual motorboat use of the calendar years 1976, 1977, and 1978 for each lake, and shall take into account the fluctuation in use during different times of the year: *Provided further*, That on each lake homeowners and their guests and resort owners and their guests on that particular lake shall have access to that particular lake and their entry shall not be counted in determining such use.

Motorboat use, entry point quotas.

(g) Nothing in this Act shall be deemed to require the termination of the existing operation of motor vehicles to assist in the transport of boats across the portages from Sucker Lake to Basswood Lake, from Fall Lake to Basswood Lake, and from Lake Vermilion to Trout Lake, during the period ending January 1, 1984. Following said date, unless the Secretary determines that there is no feasible nonmotorized means of transporting boats across the portages to reach the lakes previously served by the portages listed above, he shall terminate all such motorized use of each portage listed above.

Boat portages, motorized assistance.

127

Motorized craft, authorizations.

Additional standards and criteria.

(h) The motorized uses authorized by this section shall be confined to those types of snowmobiles, motorboats and vehicles which have been in regular use in the Boundary Waters Canoe Area prior to the date of enactment of this Act. The Secretary may set forth additional standards and criteria to further define the type of motorized craft which may be permitted.

(i) Except for motorboats, snowmobiles, and mechanized portaging, as authorized and defined herein, no other motorized use of the wilderness shall be permitted. Nothing in this Act shall prohibit the use of aircraft, motorboats, snowmobiles, or other mechanized uses in emergencies, or for the administration of the wilderness area by Federal, State, and local governmental officials or their deputies, only where the Secretary finds that such use is essential.

RESORTS

Purchase, notice from owner.

Fair market value.

SEC. 5. (a) The owner of a resort in commercial operation during 1975, 1976 or 1977 and located on land riparian to any of the lakes listed below may require purchase of that resort, including land and buildings appurtenant thereto, by written notice to the Secretary prior to September 30, 1985. The value of such resort for purposes of such sale shall be based upon its fair market value as of July 1, 1978, or as of the date of said written notice, whichever is greater, without regard to restrictions imposed by this Act:

Fall, Lake County, Moose, Lake County, Snowbank, Lake County, Lake One, Lake County, Sawbill, Cook County, Brule, Cook County, East Bearskin, Cook County, Clearwater, Cook County, Saganaga, Cook County, Sea Gull, Cook County, McFarland, Cook County, North Fowl, Cook County, South Fowl, Cook County, Jasper Lake, Lake County, Ojibway, Lake County.

Residence retention.

(b) An owner requiring purchase of a resort under this provision may elect to retain one or more appropriate buildings and lands not exceeding three acres, for personal use as a residence: *Provided,* That the purchase price to the Government for a resort shall be reduced by the fair market value of such buildings and lands, with the same valuation procedures outlined above.

(c) With respect to any privately owned lands and interests in lands riparian to the lakes listed above, and if the Federal Government has been required to purchase a resort on said lake, said lands shall not be sold without first being offered for sale to the Secretary who shall be given a period of one hundred days after the date of each such offer within which to purchase such lands. No such lands shall be sold at a price below the price at which they have been offered for sale to the Secretary, and if such lands are reoffered for sale they shall first be reoffered to the Secretary: *Provided,* That, this right of first refusal shall not apply to a change in ownership of a property within an immediate family.

Appropriation authorization.

(d) There are authorized to be appropriated such sums as may be necessary for the acquisition of lands and interests therein as provided by this section.

TIMBER SALE CONTRACTS

Termination period.

SEC. 6. (a) The Secretary is directed to terminate within a period of one year after the date of passage of this Act, all timber sale contracts in the Boundary Waters Canoe Area Wilderness. There shall be no further logging of the virgin forest areas formerly enjoined from logging by the United States District Court on said contract areas during the termination period.

128

The purpose of said termination period is only to permit completion of the harvesting of timber within existing areas under contract that are not within the areas described above and permit the taking of ameliorative measures, including land and cover restoration that will, at the earliest feasible date, make the imprint of man's work substantially unnoticeable on the lands included as wilderness in this Act.

(b)(1) In the event that termination of timber sale contracts in subsection (a) reduces the total national forest volume which a purchaser has under contract on the Superior National Forest to less than two years cut based on the average volume of Superior National Forest timber harvested by the purchaser in the last three years, the Secretary may, with the consent of the purchaser, substitute, to the extent practicable, timber on other national forest lands approximately equal in species and volume to the timber sale contract affected. In offering substitute timber, the Secretary shall negotiate the substitution at a price that is mutually equitable considering such factors as species, volume, logging accessibility, and other terms of the agreement.

Substitution.

(2) The United States will pay just compensation for any timber contracts terminated or modified by this Act, consistent with amendment V to the Constitution of the United States. Losses due to costs incurred in directly fulfilling the terms of such contracts shall be paid by the United States. Any action for the recovery from the United States of cost as provided above shall be brought in a court of competent jurisdiction. Any such judgments shall be paid from the claims and judgments fund (31 U.S.C. 724a).

Compensation.

USC prec. title 1.

Recovery.

(c) Within the limits of applicable laws and prudent forest management:

(1) the Secretary shall, in furtherance of the purposes of subsection (a) of this section and of section 4 of the National Forest Management Act of 1976 (90 Stat. 2949), expedite the intensification of resource management including emphasis on softwood timber production and hardwood utilization on the national forest lands in Minnesota outside the wilderness to offset, to the extent feasible, the reduction in the programmed allowable timber harvest resulting from reclassification of the Boundary Waters Area, and the Secretary shall make a review of progress to date in 1983, and a forecast of planned achievements by 1985 and shall submit, as a part of the 1985 program under the schedule called for in the Resources Planning Act of 1974, a Plan and recommendations for 1985–1990. In administering the Superior National Forest, the Secretary is authorized and directed to engage in artificial and natural regeneration, release, site preparation, and other forms of timber production enhancement.

Resource management review and plan.
16 USC 1601.

Administrative provisions.

(2) The Secretary, in carrying out the requirements in section (c)(1), is authorized and directed to cooperate with the State of Minnesota and its political subdivisions to develop and implement a system of grants, for the development of renewable resources on State, County and private lands. He may also seek the cooperation of other Federal departments and agencies to assure a coordinated approach to renewable resources development.

Grants system, cooperation.

(d) There is authorized to be appropriated, in addition to such sums as may otherwise be appropriated for the Superior National Forest from existing authorities established by law, the following additional sums for the fiscal years 1980 through 1990 inclusive:

Appropriation authorizations.

(1) to carry out the purposes of subsection 6(c)(1) an additional $8,000,000 annually; and,

(2) to carry out the purposes of subsection 6(c)(2) an additional $3,000,000 annually: *Provided, however,* That the Federal share of any grant made pursuant to subsection 6(c)(2) shall not exceed 80 percent of the total cost of said grant.

(e) Funds appropriated pursuant to this section shall remain available until expended. Authorizations in excess of funds appropriated in a given fiscal year shall remain available for appropriation in subsequent fiscal years.

(f) In addition to those personnel who would otherwise be available, the Secretary is authorized to appoint and fix the compensation (not to exceed that of grade 15 on the General Schedule for Federal employees) of additional full-time personnel for the Superior National Forest to carry out the purposes of this Act.

5 USC 5332 note.

LAWS APPLICABLE TO CERTAIN LANDS AND WATERS IN THE SUPERIOR NATIONAL FOREST

SEC. 7. (a) The provisions of the Acts listed in paragraph (b) of this section shall continue to apply to lands and waters specified in such Acts notwithstanding the inclusion of any such lands and waters in the wilderness or mining protection area designated under this Act. For lands and waters to which such Acts listed in paragraph (b) apply which are also within the wilderness or mining protection area designated under this Act, any withdrawal, prohibition, or restriction contained in such Acts listed in paragraph (b) shall be in addition to any withdrawal, prohibition, or restriction otherwise applicable to such wilderness or mining protection area under any other law.

(b) The Acts referred to in paragraph (a) are as follows:
(1) The Act of July 10, 1930 (46 Stat. 1020; 16 U.S.C. 577a, 577b), herein referred to as the "Shipstead-Nolan Act".
(2) The Act of June 22, 1948 (62 Stat. 568, as amended, 16 U.S.C. 577c–577b), herein referred to as the "Thye-Blatnik Act".

(c) The provisions of the Shipstead-Nolan Act are hereby extended and made applicable to all lands and waters not otherwise subject to such Act which are within the wilderness designated under this Act.

(d)(1) The authorities contained in the Thye-Blatnik Act are hereby extended and made applicable to all lands and waters not otherwise subject to such Act which are within the wilderness designated under this Act.

(2) In applying the second proviso of section 5 of such Thye-Blatnik Act to the areas to which such Act is extended and made applicable under this subsection, the phrase "fiscal year 1980" shall be substituted for the phrase "the first full fiscal year after the approval of this Act" in such proviso.

16 USC 577g.

Appropriation authorization.

(3) There are authorized to be appropriated such sums as may be necessary to carry out the provisions of the Thye-Blatnik Act with respect to the lands and waters within the wilderness designated under this Act. Such sums may be used for the payment of court judgments in condemnation actions brought under the terms of the Thye-Blatnik Act without regard to the date such condemnation actions were initially instituted. Funds appropriated from the Land and Water Conservation Fund may be used for the acquisition of any lands and waters, or interests therein within such wilderness.

EXISTING AIRSPACE RESERVATION

SEC. 8. The provisions of Executive Order 10092 as made applicable to the Boundary Waters Canoe Area established by the Wilderness Act of 1964 shall be deemed incorporated into this Act.

16 USC 1131 note.

MINING PROTECTION AREA ESTABLISHMENT

SEC. 9. In order to protect existing natural values and high standards of environmental quality from the adverse impacts associated with mineral development, there is hereby established the Boundary Waters Canoe Area Mining Protection Area (hereinafter in this Act referred to as the "mining protection area"), comprising approximately two hundred and twenty-two thousand acres.

MAP AND BOUNDARIES

SEC. 10. The mining protection area shall comprise the area generally depicted as a mining protection area on the map entitled "Boundary Waters Canoe Area Wilderness and Boundary Waters Canoe Area Mining Protection Area" dated September 1978, which shall be on file and available for public inspection in the offices of the Supervisor of the Superior National Forest and of the Chief, United States Forest Service. As soon as practicable after this Act takes effect, the Secretary shall file a map and a legal description of the mining protection area with the Committee on Interior and Insular Affairs of the House of Representatives and the Committee on Energy and Natural Resources of the United States Senate. Such map and description shall have the same force and effect as if included in this Act. Correction of clerical and typographical errors in such description may be made.

Filing with congressional committees.

MINING AND MINERAL LEASING IN THE WILDERNESS AND MINING PROTECTION AREA

SEC. 11. (a) In addition to any other applicable prohibition or withdrawal from entry or appropriation under any provision of the Wilderness Act or under any other provision of law, no permit, lease, or other authorization may be issued by any agency or authority of the United States for—

Prohibitions.

(1) exploration for, or mining of, minerals owned by the United States within the Boundary Waters Canoe Area Wilderness and Boundary Waters Canoe Area Mining Protection Area; or

(2) exploration for, or mining of minerals within such areas if such activities may affect navigable waters; or

(3) the use of property owned by the United States in relation to any mining of or exploration for minerals in such areas which may materially impair the wilderness qualities of the wilderness area or which may materially impair the natural values and environmental quality of the mining protection area.

The prohibitions contained in this subsection and any withdrawal from entry or appropriation for mining of or exploration for minerals applicable to the Boundary Waters Canoe Area Wilderness and Boundary Waters Canoe Area Mining Protection Area shall not apply to the extent specifically provided in legislation enacted by the United States after the date of enactment of this Act pursuant to a national emergency declared by the President.

(b) (1) Consistent with the prohibitions and other requirements in subsection (a) of this section, no permit, lease, or other authorization shall be issued unless and until—

(A) the Secretary shall have approved a plan that details how mining will be conducted consistent with this Act and with other Federal, State, and local requirements, and that details how the area will be restored to its original condition or to a substantially equivalent condition, including the estimated cost thereof;

(B) the applicant has posted a bond for performance payable to the United States in an amount determined by the Secretary to be sufficient to assure completion of the reclamation plan if the work had to be performed by the United States;

(C) the applicant shall have obtained all permits, licenses, certifications, and approvals required by Federal, State, or local law; and (iv) the Secretary has determined that no permanent facility will be constructed nor alteration will occur that could render the area incapable of reverting to its original condition or to a substantially equivalent condition.

(2) The provisions of paragraphs (2) and (3) of section 4(d) of the Wilderness Act (78 Stat. 890; 16 U.S.C. 1133(d)(2) and 16 U.S.C. 1133(d)(3)) shall not apply to the area designated herein as the Boundary Waters Canoe Area Wilderness.

Minerals or mineral rights, acquisition.

(c) The Secretary is authorized to acquire any minerals or mineral rights within the wilderness and mining protection area alleged to be owned by persons other than the Federal or State governments in the following manner:

(1) The Secretary first may seek to acquire these minerals or mineral rights by donation. In seeking a donation, the Secretary shall inform the person alleging the ownership interest of the procedures and limitations to be followed in acquisition by purchase as set forth in paragraph (2) below.

(2) If the person alleging the ownership interest does not donate his minerals or mineral rights to either the Federal or State governments, the Secretary is authorized to acquire the rights by purchase, within the limits of funds appropriated for property acquisition in the Superior National Forest, and in an amount appropriately discounted for the following factors if existent in relation to the particular mineral interest:

(A) The original patenting from the Federal public domain was fraudulent. The patenting of lands in the Boundary Waters Canoe Area Wilderness and Boundary Waters Canoe Area Mining Protection Area is prima facie fraudulent if (1) the Act under which the patent was issued was one of the Acts intended to put settlers on the land, such as, but without limitation, the Cash Purchase Act of 1820 (chapter LI, Act of April 24, 1820, 3 U.S. Stat. 566, 567, as amended); the Preemption Act of 1830 (chapter CCVIII, Act of May 29, 1830, 4 U.S. Stat. 420, 421, as amended); the Homestead Act of 1862 (chapter LXXV, Act of May 20, 1862, 12 U.S. Stat. 392-394, as amended); and the Timber and Stone Act (chapter 150, Act of June 3, 1878, 20 U.S. Stat. 88, 89, as amended, particularly by chapter 375, Act of August 4, 1892, 27 U.S. Stat. 348); and (2) the land was patented after 1875 and before the establishment of the Superior National Forest by proclamation on February 13, 1909. The Secretary also shall consider any other evidence of fraud when determining the value of the minerals such as (1) the transfer by the entryman or patentee of whole or partial interests in the property during the patenting process or soon thereafter, (2) the appearance in the chain of title of persons known to have participated in land speculation as land brokers, entrymen, or in other capacities.

(B) The date of separation of the mineral or mineral rights from the surface interest, if the separation occurred after 1927, the year when the courts have determined that the roadless policy was established by the Secretary for the area.

(C) Any other factor, such as restrictions on mining within the area imposed by State or local government, or by operation of treaty.

(d) In the event any legal action or proceeding is instituted by or against the United States in relation to minerals or mineral rights where the patenting is prima facie fraudulent as described in subsection (c) of this section, the Attorney General of the United States shall assert the public's equitable right to constructive or public trusts, or to recover or offset damages including but not limited to those based on the value of land fraudulently acquired plus interest at 6 per centum per annum.

(e) Notwithstanding any requirement of this section, the Secretary shall have authority to acquire within the wilderness or mining protection area designated by this Act, existing mineral interests by donation, purchase, exchange, or through exercise of the power of eminent domain.

(f) There is authorized to be appropriated to the Secretary such sums as may be required to carry out the purposes of this section, to be available until expended. **Appropriation authorization.**

SEVERABILITY

SEC. 12. If any provision of this Act is declared to be invalid, such declaration shall not affect the validity of any other provision hereof.

EXISTING STRUCTURES

SEC. 13. Nothing in this Act or the Wilderness Act shall be construed to prohibit the maintenance of the Prairie Portage Dam (on the international boundary chain between Birch and Basswood Lakes), and the Secretary is authorized to perform such maintenance work as may be required to keep that dam functional at its present height and width. The Secretary is authorized to maintain other existing water control structures only where such structures are necessary to protect wilderness values or public safety. **16 USC 1131 note.**

JURISDICTION OVER FISH AND WILDLIFE

SEC. 14. Nothing in this Act shall be construed as affecting the jurisdiction or responsibilities of the State with respect to fish and wildlife in the wilderness and the mining protection area.

JURISDICTION OVER WATERS

SEC. 15. The Secretary is authorized to promulgate and enforce regulations that limit or prohibit the use of motorized equipment on or relating to waters located within the wilderness in accordance with the provisions of this Act: *Provided*, That nothing in this Act shall be construed as affecting the jurisdiction or responsibilities of the State with respect to such waters except to the extent that the exercise of such jurisdiction is less stringent than the Secretary's regulations promulgated pursuant to this section: *Provided further*, That any regulations adopted pursuant to this Act shall be complementary to, and not in derogation of regulations issued by the United States Coast Guard. **Regulations.**

Cooperative
agreements.

The Secretary is authorized to enter into cooperative agreements with the State of Minnesota with respect to enforcement of Federal and State regulations affecting the wilderness and the mining protection area.

COOPERATION WITH STATE

Administration of
mining protection
area and adjacent
lands.

SEC. 16. (a) The Secretary shall cooperate with the State of Minnesota and any political subdivision thereof in the administration of the mining protection area and in the administration and protection of lands within or adjacent to the mining protection area owned or controlled by the State or any political subdivision thereof. Nothing in this title shall deprive the State of Minnesota or any political subdivision thereof of its right to exercise civil and criminal jurisdiction within the wilderness and the mining protection area and impose land use controls and environmental health standards on non-Federal areas within the wilderness and the mining protection area, or of its right to tax persons, corporations, franchises, or other non-Federal property, including mineral or other interests, in or on lands or waters within the wilderness and the mining protection area.

(b) The Secretary is authorized to enter into cooperative agreements with the State of Minnesota with respect to enforcement of Federal and State regulations affecting the wilderness and the mining protection and shall consult with the State of Minnesota in an effort to enhance the multiple-use benefits to be derived from both State and national forest lands.

TREATIES

SEC. 17. Nothing in this Act shall affect the provisions of any treaty now applicable to lands and waters which are included in the mining protection area and the wilderness.

EXPANSION OF RECREATION PROGRAMS

SEC. 18. (a) The Secretary is authorized and directed to expedite and intensify the program of dispersed outdoor recreation development on the Superior National Forest outside the Boundary Waters Canoe Area Wilderness, as designated by this Act. The Secretary shall consider in such new program development the need for the following: additional snowmobile trails, particularly those now planned or under construction; remote campsites on lightly developed lakes; and lake access sites and parking facilities to provide motorized recreation experiences similar to those previously available in the Boundary Waters Canoe Area.

16 USC 1131
note.

(b) The Secretary, consistent with the Wilderness Act of 1964 and with this Act, is authorized to construct a system of new hiking, backpacking and cross-country ski trails within the Boundary Waters Canoe Area Wilderness as designated by this Act, and on appropriate adjacent Federal lands outside the wilderness. In constructing such a trail system, consideration should be given to locating portions of the system near existing resorts on the perimeter of the wilderness to provide additional outdoor recreation opportunities for resort guests.

(c) The Secretary is authorized and directed to develop an educational program for the recreational users of the wilderness which will assist them to understand the purpose, value, and appropriate use of wilderness lands and the functioning of natural ecosystems in wilderness.

Program for
disabled persons.

(d) The Secretary in cooperation with the State of Minnesota and other appropriate groups, consistent with the purposes of this Act, is authorized and directed to develop a program providing opportunities for a wide range of outdoor experiences for disabled persons.

(e) There are authorized to be appropriated such sums as may be necessary for the Secretary to carry out the purposes of this section.   **Appropriation authorization.**

SEC. 19. (a) The Secretary, in cooperation with other appropriate executive agencies, is authorized and directed to develop a cooperative program of technical and financial assistance to resorts in commercial operation in 1975, 1976, and 1977, and outfitters in commercial operation in 1977 which are located within the mining protection area or which are located on land adjacent to any of the lakes listed in section 5 of this Act. There are authorized to be appropriated such sums as may be necessary for the purposes of this subsection.   **Technical and financial assistance for certain commercial operations.**

(b) There are authorized to be appropriated to the Secretary funds to be made available as grants to the Agricultural Extension Service, University of Minnesota, to provide over a three-year period educational and technical assistance to businesses and communities adjacent to the Boundary Waters Canoe Area Wilderness in order to improve economic opportunities for tourism and recreation-related businesses in a manner which is complementary to the management of the wilderness.   **Grants.**

MANAGEMENT STUDY

SEC. 20. The Secretary, acting through the Chief, United States Forest Service, shall, not later than October 1, 1981, submit to the Committee on Interior and Insular Affairs of the House of Representatives and the Committee on Energy and Natural Resources of the Senate, a comprehensive management plan setting forth the specific management procedures to implement the objectives of this Act. An interim report setting forth public involvement procedures, management alternatives, and a timetable for the remaining study actions, shall be submitted within one year from the date of enactment of this Act.   **Submittal to congressional committees.**   **Interim report.**

LIMITATION OF AUTHORIZATIONS

SEC. 21. All authorizations for any funds to be appropriated under the terms of this Act shall not be effective until October 1, 1979. Notwithstanding any other provision of this Act, authority to enter into agreements or to make payments under this Act shall be effective only to the extent or in such amounts as are provided in advance in appropriation Acts.

Approved October 21, 1978.

LEGISLATIVE HISTORY:

HOUSE REPORTS: No. 95-1117, Pt. I (Comm. on Interior and Insular Affairs) and No. 95-1790 (Comm. of Conference).
SENATE REPORTS: No. 95-1274 (Comm. on Energy and Natural Resources) and No. 95-1327 (Comm. of Conference).
CONGRESSIONAL RECORD, Vol. 124 (1978):
    June 5, considered and passed House.
    Oct. 9, considered and passed Senate, amended.
    Oct. 15, House and Senate agreed to conference report.

NOTES

CHAPTER 2

1. Robert Beymer, *The Boundary Waters Canoe Area,* (Berkeley, Calif: The Wilderness Press, 1979), vol. 2, *The Eastern Region,* 4.

2. Forest Service, U.S. Department of Agriculture, *Boundary Waters Canoe Area Management Plan and Environmental Statement* (Washington, D.C.: GPO, 28 June 1974), 20. Hereafter cited as USDA-FS-R9-FES-Adm-74-1. See also Clifford and Isabel Ahlgren, *Lob Trees in the Wilderness* (Minneapolis: University of Minnesota Press, 1984), 18.

3. William J. Peterson, "Coming of the Caribou," *The Minnesota Volunteer* 44 (November–December 1981): 17–22. In the same issue, see also Harry Drabik, "You Saw a What?", 22–25.

4. For a discussion of the role of fire in managing wilderness areas, see Miron L. Heinselman, "Fire in Wilderness Ecosystems," in *Wilderness Management,* ed. John C. Hendee et al. (Washington, D.C.: U.S. Forest Service, Miscellaneous Publication No. 1365, 1978), 260–262.

5. USDA-FS-R9-FES-Adm-74-1, p. 20.

6. Ontario Ministry of Culture and Recreation, *The Archaeology of North Central Ontario: Prehistoric Cultures North of Superior* (Toronto: Field Notes, pamphlet, 1979), 4–6.

7. Ahlgren, *Lob Trees in the Wilderness,* 80.

8. Newell R. Searle, *Saving Quetico-Superior: A Land Set Apart* (St. Paul: Minnesota Historical Society Press, 1977), 4.

9. Ibid., 5.

10. Grace Lee Nute, *The Voyageur's Highway: Minnesota's Border Lake Land* (St. Paul: Minnesota Historical Society Press, 1941), 6.

11. Robert V. Bartlett, *The Reserve Mining Controversy: Science, Technology, and Environmental Policy* (Bloomington: Indiana University Press, 1980), 19.

12. USDA-FS-R9-FES-Adm-74-1, p.39. 36 Stat. 2448. The treaty defines boundary waters as the lakes and rivers between the borders of the two nations, "including all bays, arms, and inlets thereof." Rivers and streams flowing into boundary waters are not included.

13. Searle, *Saving Quetico-Superior,* 50.

14. Ibid., 70.

15. USDA-FS-R9-FES-Adm-74-1, p. 62.

16. Searle, *Saving Quetico-Superior,* 31.

17. USDA-FS-R9-FES-Adm-74-1, pp. 36–37.

18. 46 Stat. 1020. P.L. 71-539. See also chapter 4 in Searle, *Saving Quetico-Superior,* for a detailed account of the statute.

138 NOTES TO PAGES 18–26

19. 62 Stat. 568. P.L. 80-733. See Searle, *Saving Quetico-Superior,* chapter 7.

20. Roderick Nash, *Wilderness and the American Mind,* 3d ed. (New Haven, Conn.: Yale University Press, 1982), 324. See also chapter 9 in Hendee et al., *Wilderness Management.*

21. L. C. Merriam, Jr., and C. K. Smith, "Visitor Impact on Newly Developed Campsites in the Boundary Waters Canoe Area," *Journal of Forestry* 72 (Summer 1974): 627–30.

22. Donald N. Baldwin, *The Quiet Revolution: Grass Roots of Today's Wilderness Preservation Movement* (Boulder, Colo: Pruett Publishing Co., 1972), 101. The author calls Carhart's action "the first de facto application of the wilderness concept."

23. Hendee, et al., *Wilderness Management,* 61–62.

24. Ibid., 62–63.

25. Frank C. Keyser, *The Preservation of Wilderness Areas: An Analysis of Opinion on the Problem* (Washington, D.C.: Legislative Reference Service, Library of Congress, 1949).

26. 78 Stat. 891. P.L. 88-577. See also Michael McCloskey, "The Wilderness Act of 1964: Its Background and Meaning," *Oregon Law Review* 45 (April 1966): 298.

27. 88 Stat. 2069. P.L. 93-622.

28. James Weaver and Malcom Rupert Cutler, "Wilderness Policy: A Colloquy between Congressman Weaver and Assistant Secretary Cutler," *Journal of Forestry* 75 (July 1977): 392–93.

29. *Izaak Walton League of America v. St. Clair,* 313 F. Supp. 1312 (D. Minn., 1970).

30. Ibid., 353 F. Supp. 714–15.

31. Kevin Haight, "The Wilderness Act: Ten Years After," *Environmental Affairs* 3 (1974): 295.

32. *Minnesota Public Interest Research Group v. Butz,* 358 F. Supp. 584 (D. Minn. 1973).

33. Ibid., 629.

34. Ibid., 541 F. 2d 1292 (8th Circuit, 1976).

35. Robert Cary, managing editor, *Ely Echo,* interview with author, Ely, Minnesota, 4 August 1983, transcript, 12. Cary noted that the congressman agreed to the moratorium before consulting the Kainz Logging Company.

36. Delbert V. Mecure, Jr., and William M. Ross, "The Wilderness Act: A Product of Congressional Compromise," in *Congress and the Environment,* ed. Richard A. Cooley and Geoffrey Wandesford-Smith (Seattle: University of Washington Press, 1970), 47–64.

37. See Malcom Rupert Cutler, "A Study of Litigation Related to Management of Forest Service Administered Lands and its Effect on Policy Decisions. Part Two: A Comparison of Four Cases" (Ph.D. Diss., Michigan State University, 1972). Among other cases, the author examines efforts by George St. Clair to begin mining in the BWCA, which resulted in litigation.

CHAPTER 3

1. Searle, *Saving Quetico-Superior,* 24.

2. Ibid., 144.

3. *Perko v. U.S.,* F. 2d 446 (8th Circuit, 1953). See Searle, *Saving Quetico-Superior,* 185.

4. Ibid., 166.

5. Ibid.

6. *Mesabi Daily News,* 18 February 1958.

7. Ibid.

8. *Duluth News-Tribune,* 20 July 1957. The reasons against the wilderness bill were similar to those found in a February 1956 resolution by the commissioners of Saint Louis and Lake counties opposing a bill to appropriate federal money to implement the Thye-Blatnik Act of 1948. The commissioners condemned the bill, which would have called for the purchase of more inholdings, as "an encroachment upon the economy of the area and too restrictive of access to the wilderness area." The bill was to appropriate over two million dollars to acquire private lands within the area and purchase additional lands outside the area. The commissioners asserted that this would eliminate more private property from county tax rolls and further shrink revenues needed by local governments to provide public services. See also *Duluth News-Tribune,* 28 February 1956.

9. *Duluth News-Tribune,* 20 July 1957.

10. Ibid.

11. Ibid. See *Ely Miner,* 17 July 1957.

12. *Duluth News-Tribune,* 27 July 1957. Senator Humphrey's rationale did not explain why the BWCA was to be included in a wilderness system when no management changes were to take place.

13. Ibid.

14. Ibid.

15. *Mesabi Daily News,* 1 February 1961.

16. U.S. Congress, Senate, Committee on Interior and Insular Affairs, *Hearings on S. 1176,* 85th Cong., 1st sess., 19-20 June 1957, 100. See also *Duluth News-Tribune,* 20 July 1957.

17. *Mesabi Daily News,* 11 December 1957.

18. Ibid., 7 December 1957.

19. *Senator Hubert H. Humphrey's Informal Hearing on Senate File No. S. 1176, Known as the Wilderness Bill,* transcript of hearing held in St. Paul on 11 December 1957, Christopher Columbus and Associates, Court Reporters, 38-40. From the files of Brian O'Neill, attorney, Faegre and Benson, Minneapolis, Minn.

20. Ibid., 45. In introducing his second wilderness bill on the Boundary Waters, Senator Humphrey stated, "This bill will not interfere with, but will perpetuate, the present multiple-purpose administration of these national forest areas." 103 *Congressional Record* 1894 (11 February 1957).

21. Wesley J. White, *The Selke Review Committee,* Historical Files of the Superior National Forest, Duluth, Minn., 1971, 1, Charles Dayton Papers, Box 13, Archives/Manuscripts Division of the Minnesota Historical Society, St. Paul. (Minnesota Historical Society is hereafter cited as MHS.)

22. Ibid., 1-2.

23. *Duluth News-Tribune,* 10 May 1964.

24. Ibid., 6 June 1964.

25. Ibid., 22 June 1964.

26. White, *The Selke Review Committee,* 3.

27. Ibid., 4. White observed that snowmobile use was against Forest Service wilderness policy, as it was a form of mechanized recreation. But he also noted the problematic nature of the BWCA case: it was managed as a semiwilderness area in which the nonwilderness uses of logging and motorized recreation were allowed. See

Wesley J. White, *History Involved in the Decisions to Set Up Winter Snowmobile Routes,* 1973, 1, Charles Dayton Papers, Box 13, MHS.

28. *Mesabi Daily News,* 11 July 1964.

29. *Duluth News-Tribune,* 13 January 1965.

30. Ibid., 21 January 1965.

31. Ibid.

32. *Duluth Herald,* 28 January 1965.

33. *Duluth News-Tribune,* 2 February 1965.

34. Ibid., 3 March 1965.

35. *Duluth Herald,* 29 June 1965.

36. Northeastern Minnesota Development Association, "Economic Effects of Proposed Management Changes in the Boundary Waters Canoe Area," prepared for the Boundary Waters Resources Committee of the Minnesota Arrowhead Association (Duluth, Minn.: August 1965) iv.

37. Boundary Waters Resources Committee, "Recreational Studies in Correlation with Forest Management and Local Area Economy" (September 1965) 1.

38. *Duluth Herald,* 25 August 1965. Trygg also accused preservationists of "clever, but not factual propaganda" to get the high-level BWCA review committee established. See *Duluth News-Tribune,* 3 March 1965. Robert Cary, a newspaper reporter from Chicago, asserted: "The U.S. public has been told erroneously that foresters are overcutting and spoiling the entire wilderness area, and the local people here have no means of defending themselves or altering this impression." *Duluth News-Tribune,* 24 January 1965.

39. *Duluth News-Tribune,* 17 December 1965.

40. Ibid.

41. USDA-FS-R9-FES-Adm-74-1, P-35.

42. Correspondence between Jay H. Cravens, Regional Forester, Eastern Region and Charles K. Dayton, attorney for Minnesota Federation of Ski Touring Clubs on request for administrative review of Land Use Management Plan for the Boundary Waters Canoe Area, Superior National Forest, 16 September 1974, Charles Dayton Papers, Box 14, MHS.

43. Ibid.

44. Environmental Law Review 7:20531.

45. *Duluth News-Tribune,* 7 May 1975.

46. Ibid., 15 May 1975.

47. Ibid., 1 June 1975.

48. Ibid., 17 May 1975.

49. Ibid.

50. Ibid., 17 June 1975.

51. Ibid., 15 June 1975.

52. Ibid., 16 October 1975.

53. *Environmental Law Review* 7:20533.

54. *Duluth Herald,* 22 April 1976. In 1941 the Forest Service established two zones in the canoe area, the Portal and Interior Zones. No timber cutting was allowed in the Interior Zone, but the agency could permit cutting in the Portal Zone at its discretion, provided that it did not permit logging within four hundred feet of shorelines.

55. *Duluth News-Tribune,* 18 April 1976.

56. Ibid.

57. Ibid., 23 April 1976. For a similar argument, see William Tucker, "Environmentalism and the Leisure Class," *Harper's* 225 (December 1977): 49–80. Tucker ex-

pands this argument in *Progress and Privilege: America in the Age of Environmentalism* (Garden City, N.Y.: Anchor Press-Doubleday, 1982). He argues that a privileged class of Americans manipulate the political system in the name of environmentalism to block economic progress and thereby to protect the class's social status. Tucker refers to the BWCA motor issue but does not develop an analysis of the problem.

58. *Duluth News-Tribune,* 23 April 1976. The Arrowhead Region is a wedge of land in northeastern Minnesota. It is bordered by Lake Superior to the south and by the Canadian province of Ontario to the north.

59. *Environmental Law Review* 7:20533.

60. Ibid. For a copy of the executive order, see David Sheridan, *Off-Road Vehicles on the Public Lands* (Washington, D.C.: GPO, 1979), 68–69.

61. *Environmental Law Review* 7:20533.

62. Ibid.

63. *Environmental Law Review* 7:20534.

64. *Duluth Herald,* 20 January 1977.

65. *Wilderness News* (Quetico-Superior Foundation), Fall 1973, 2.

CHAPTER 4

1. Charles Dayton, Letter to author, 2 April 1984, BWCA files, Department of Political Science/Justice, University of Alaska Fairbanks.

2. *Duluth News-Tribune,* 16 October 1975.

3. *Minneapolis Star,* 16 October 1975.

4. Ibid.

5. *Wilderness News* (Quetico-Superior Foundation), Spring 1976, 1.

6. *Duluth Herald,* 2 March 1976.

7. Ibid.

8. Miron Heinselman, former chairman of the Friends, interview with author, Ely, Minn., 2 August 1983, transcript, 2.

9. *Your Boundary Waters Canoe Area Wilderness Needs Help, Now,* Ely, Minn., 2 August 1983.

10. David W. Lime, "Sources of Congestion and Visitor Dissatisfaction in the Boundary Waters Canoe Area," in *Proceedings, the Quetico-Superior Foundation 1975 Institute on the Boundary Waters Canoe Area,* Duluth, Minn., 9 May 1975 (Minneapolis, Minn.: Quetico-Superior Foundation).

11. 123 *Congressional Record* H621 (31 January 1977).

12. Richard Rapson, a legislative aide on Fraser's staff, referred to Fraser's total wilderness bill as "staking out our philosophical ground as clearly as we could." See Richard Rapson, attorney, Leonard, Street, and Deinard, interview with author, Minneapolis, Minn., 27 July 1983, transcript, 10.

13. Bill Cunningham, vice-chairman of the Friends, identified these two sources of membership. See *Ely Echo,* 18 May 1977. Charles Dayton also noted that the Friends used the Freedom of Information Act to obtain BWCA visitor data from permits issued by the Forest Service. These permits contained the names, addresses, and method of travel of those who entered the canoe area. The Friends mailed its literature to those who had visited the area and who had traveled by canoe and thus was able to increase its membership.

14. *Duluth News-Tribune,* 15 October 1977.

15. *Ely Echo,* 1 June 1977.

16. *Duluth News-Tribune,* 16 June 1977.

17. Sheila Ballavance, former Alliance treasurer, interview with author, Duluth, Minn., 29 July 1983, transcript, 15.

18. *Duluth News-Tribune,* 3 June 1977.

19. Ibid.

20. *St. Paul Pioneer Press,* 9 March 1977.

21. *Ely Echo,* 8 July 1977.

22. Ibid.

23. Ibid., 6 July 1977.

24. Ibid.

25. Ibid., 8 June 1977. The Minnesota Eighth District Republicans in May 1977 had called for a fact-finding commission a month earlier in order to examine BWCA management issues. They claimed that a qualified committee of experts had not reviewed either bill, referring to the Selke committee's recommendation in 1964 that another commission should be formed in the event that new management rules were proposed. The party resolution called for an "immediate moratorium on the two BWCA bills now before Congress until a study committee of eminent authorities are appointed." See *Ely Echo,* 11 May 1977.

26. *Ely Echo,* 8 June 1977.

27. *Duluth News-Tribune,* 9 July 1977.

28. *Ely Echo,* 13 July 1977.

29. Ibid., 20 July 1977.

30. Ibid. 27 July 1977.

31. For a summary of the opinion poll, see the *Duluth News-Tribune,* 15 August 1977. In 1978 a second statewide survey was conducted. It found that 58 percent of those surveyed supported "legislation that sharply curtails motorized vehicles," while 38 percent wanted "a bill that permits greater use of motorboats and snowmobiles." The poll showed a shift in support for the Friends position. See the *Minnesota Tribune,* 16 July 1978. Respondents were asked in the survey to list their level of education, type of work, and other personal information. The data collected supports the thesis that the political goals of environmentalists are more likely to be favored by the upper-middle class. See Joseph Harry et al., "Conservation: An Upper Middle Class Social Movement," *Journal of Leisure Research* 1 (Summer 1969): 246–54. See also John C. Hendee et al., "Conservation, Politics, and Democracy," *Journal of Soil and Water Conservation* 24 (November–December 1969): 212–15.

32. *Newsletter—Washington Action Alert* (Friends of the Boundary Waters Wilderness), September 1977, 2.

33. See U.S. Congress, House Subcommittee on National Parks and Insular Affairs, *Legislative History of the Boundary Waters Canoe Area Wilderness Act (Public Law 95-495),* 95th Cong., 2d sess., 1979, Committee Print 10, 10.

34. *Duluth Herald,* 13 September 1977.

35. Irvin Anderson, testimony before House Subcommittee hearings on H.R. 2820 and H.R. 8722, Washington, D.C., 12–13 September 1977, 2, BWCA files, Environmental Conservation Library, Minneapolis Public Library. (Hereafter cited as ECOL.)

36. In *United States v. Brown,* 522 F. 2d 817 (8th Circuit, 1977), the defendant claimed that federal regulations prohibiting hunting in Voyageurs National Park were unconstitutional; the state government held jurisdiction over the waters on which he hunted. The court ruled, however, that "the property clause authorized federal regula-

tion of hunting on the state-owned lakes." It acknowledged the authority of Congress to regulate nonfederal property in cases where failure to do so would frustrate legislative intent. See Eugene R. Gaetke, "The Boundary Waters Canoe Area Wilderness Act of 1978: Regulating Nonfederal Property Under the Property Clause," *Oregon Law Review* 60 (1981): 178–80. The same reasoning was later applied to support the authority of Congress for regulating motorized travel on BWCA waters.

37. Mathew Kaufman, testimony before House Subcommittee hearings, 12 September 1977, 1, Charles Dayton Papers, Box 15, MHS. Kaufman's testimony was similar to comments made by the president of the Far West Ski Association (FWSA) on a Forest Service EIS. See U.S. Department of Agriculture, *The 1980 Report to the Congress on the Nation's Renewable Resources* (Washington, D.C.: GPO, 1980), 89–98. Kaufman argued that designating more wilderness areas on federal lands unfairly precluded other types of recreation. The president of the FWSA contended that the supply of alpine skiing areas on public lands did not meet current demand levels because of "over-reaction by extreme environmentalists." He asserted that "there simply must be a recognition of the values of developed recreation" on public lands administered by the Forest Service.

38. Kaufman testimony, 3.

39. Senator Church, as a member of the Senate Interior and Insular Affairs Committee, had been active in efforts to pass the Wilderness Act of 1964. Maintaining that strict, purist standards for wilderness management were contrary to the statute, he asserted: "If Congress had intended that wilderness be administered in so stringent a manner, we would have never written the law as we did . . . we wouldn't have provided for the continuation of nonconforming uses where they were established . . . including the use of motorboats in parts of the Boundary Waters Canoe Area." See Frank Church, "Wither Wilderness," *American Forests* 83 (July 1977): 11–12, 38–41.

40. Kaufman testimony, 10.

41. Janet C. Green, testimony before House Subcommittee hearings, 12 September 1977, 14, Charles Dayton Papers, Box 15, MHS.

42. Ibid., 25.

43. Timothy B. Knopp, testimony before House Subcommittee hearings, 12 September 1977, 1 BWCA files, ECOL. See John Baden, "Neospartan Hedonists, Adult Toy Aficionados, and Public Lands," in *Managing the Commons,* ed. Garrett Hardin and John Baden (San Francisco: W. H. Freeman and Company, 1977), 244. Baden argues that visitors who use motors will obtain a a virtual monopoly over an area, while nonmotorists will be driven out because the noise bothers them.

44. Knopp testimony, 1. See Garrett Hardin, "The Economics of Wilderness," *Natural History* 78 (June 1969): 20–7. Hardin argues that travel from the edge to the center of a wilderness area is an intrinsic part of the experience.

45. Knopp testimony, 2.

46. Ibid.

47. William Muir, testimony before House Subcommittee hearings, 11 September 1977, 3, BWCA files, ECOL.

48. *Duluth News-Tribune,* 14 September 1977.

49. *Duluth Herald,* 15 September 1977.

50. *Minneapolis Star,* 4 November 1977.

51. Russell Brown, "The Loci of Conflict and Compromise: Preservation and Consumption," in *Vital Speeches* 37 (February 1971): 248–49.

52. S. F. Cotgrove, *Catastrophe or Cornucopia: The Environment, Politics, and the Future* (Chichester, N.Y.: John Wiley and Sons, 1982), 33.

53. See Baden, "Neospartan Hedonists," 244. Baden argues that users can be expected "to ignore the adverse effect of their action upon others." Because the disturbance is only one-way, motor users often cannot, or will not, acknowledge that motors irritate visitors who prefer to travel without motors.

CHAPTER 5

1. *Duluth News-Tribune,* 17 March 1978.
2. Ibid., 18 March 1978.
3. Ibid.
4. Ibid., 26 March 1978.
5. Ibid. The Alliance was not alone in its concern over the issue of water jurisdiction. Shortly after the Burton-Vento bill (H.R. 12250) was announced, William Nye, commissioner of the Minnesota Department of Natural Resources, testified before the House Subcommittee on Parks and Insular Affairs. He emphasized the state's concern over federal regulations for water travel in the wilderness area, asserting that these measures would "strip Minnesota of its water rights in the BWCA." Burton stated that he would consider making changes in the subcommittee bill but pointed out that it was written to acknowledge the right of Minnesota "to set more stringent regulations on BWCA users." Nye took a dim view of this assurance, comparing it to the right "to limit canoes to one paddle instead of two." *Duluth News-Tribune,* 4 April 1978.
6. Ibid., 2 April 1978.
7. Ibid., 6 April 1978.
8. Ibid., 5 April 1978.
9. Ibid.
10. Friends of the Boundary Waters Wilderness Newsletter, 20 April 1978, 3–4.
11. *Duluth News-Tribune,* 12 April 1978.
12. We are fighting for the Spirit of '64 (Boundary Waters Conservation Alliance), undated pamphlet, BWCA files, ECOL. For a similar criticism of Forest Service wilderness management policy, see Ted Trueblood, "The Forest Service Versus the Wilderness Act," *Field and Stream* 80 (September 1975): 16, 18, 40. See also Allan May, *Voice in the Wilderness* (Chicago: Nelson-Hall, Inc., 1978).
13. *Spirit of '64.*
14. *Duluth News-Tribune,* 8 April 1978.
15. Bruce Kerfoot, owner, Gunflint Lodge, interview with author, Gunflint Trail, Minn., 31 July 1983, transcript, 52.
16. *Voices in the Wilderness* (Boundary Waters Conservation Alliance) June 1978, 1.
17. Ibid.
18. Richard Rapson, a legislative aide to Fraser, argued that the best strategy for passing a wilderness-oriented bill was to make compromises in H.R. 12250 before it reached the House floor. Other wilderness supporters disagreed, arguing that the bill had enough support to pass a floor vote without amendments that would weaken it. See Richard Rapson, attorney, Leonard, Street, and Deinard, interview with author, Minneapolis, Minn., 27 July 1983, transcript, 18–20.
19. *Minneapolis Tribune,* 31 May 1978.
20. Ibid.
21. 124 *Congressional Record* H4944 (5 June 1978).
22. Ibid., H4945.

23. Ibid.

24. Ibid., S9638 (23 June 1978).

25. *Duluth News-Tribune,* 24 June 1978.

26. U.S. Congress, Senate Subcommittee on Parks and Recreation, Committee on Energy and Natural Resources, *BWCA Wilderness and Mining Protection Area, Hearing on S. 3242 and H.R. 12250,* 95th Cong., 2d sess. 17 August 1978, 71.

27. Ibid.

28. Ibid., 69.

29. Ibid.

30. *Minneapolis Tribune,* 31 July 1978.

31. Ibid., 18 August 1978.

32. Ibid.

33. Ibid., 6 August 1978.

34. Ibid., 18 August 1978.

35. 124 *Congressional Record* H13440 (14 October 1978).

36. Ibid., H13443.

37. Ibid. Robert Short defeated Fraser in the September primaries, but Short lost the general election to his Republican opponent, David Durenburger. The Alliance attributed Fraser's defeat to the BWCA issue. Wendell Anderson lost his election bid to Rudy Boschwitz.

38. Sheila Ballavance, former Alliance treasurer, interview with author, Duluth, Minn., 29 July 1983, transcript, 15.

39. Robert Cary, ed., *Ely Echo,* interview with author, Ely, Minn., 4 August 1983, transcript, 24–5.

40. See Eric Ashby, *Reconciling Man with the Environment* (Stanford, Calif.: Stanford University Press, 1978), 5. Ashby argues that a new ethic toward nature is emerging in modern civilization. He notes that "primitive man identified himself with the environment through the beliefs of animism; modern man is against identifying himself with the environment, this time through the evidence of science."

CHAPTER 6

1. *Duluth News-Tribune,* 16 October 1978.

2. Ibid., 17 October 1978.

3. Ibid., 10 November 1978.

4. Ibid., 9 December 1978.

5. *Ely Miner,* 4 April 1979.

6. For a similar idea, see Lynn White, Jr., "The Historical Roots of Our Ecologic Crisis," *Science* 155 (10 March 1976): 1203–7. See also John Passmore, *Man's Responsibility for Nature: Ecological Problems and Western Traditions* (Surrey, England: Gresham Press, 1974).

7. *U.S. v. Brown,* 552 F. 2d 821 (8th Circuit, 1977). For an analysis of the federal property clause, see Eugene Gaetke, "The Boundary Waters Canoe Area Wilderness Act of 1978: Regulating Nonfederal Property Under the Property Clause," *Oregon Law Review* 60 (1981): 157–83. See also Gaetke, "Congressional Discretion Under the Property Clause," *Hastings Law Journal* 33 (November 1981): 381–402.

8. Gaetke, "The Boundary Waters Act," 179. The property clause states, "The Congress shall have power to dispose of and make all needful Rules and Regulations respecting the Territory or other Property belonging to the United States." Given the

U.S. v. Brown decision, Attorney General Warren Spannus (an elected official) refused to litigate the water rights case because there appeared to be little chance of success. The state retained Wayne Olson as special counsel to bring the lawsuit; he was a former commissioner of the Department of Conservation and a member of the Selke committee. See *Minneapolis Tribune,* 23 December 1979.

9. See Brian O'Neill et al., *Judicial, Legislative and Administrative Chronology,* prepared for *Minnesota v. Bergland,* U.S. District Court, Duluth, Minn., Civil No. 5-79-178, 61. Obtained from the files of Brian O'Neill, Faegre and Benson, Minneapolis, Minn.

10. See "Statement of the Commissioner of Natural Resources Joseph N. Alexander Regarding the State of Minnesota's Litigation Concerning Assertion by the Federal Government of Jurisdiction over Certain of the Public Waters Located Within the Superior National Forest." 20 April 1979, 3–4. BWCA Papers, MHS.

11. *St. Paul Pioneer Press,* 13 April 1979.

12. *Ely Echo,* 30 April 1979. In late 1979 U.S. Senator-elect David Durenberger pointed out that continued resistance to implementing P.L. 95-495 might jeopardize federal appropriations. See *Minneapolis Tribune,* 23 December 1979.

13. *Duluth News-Tribune,* 13 April 1979.

14. *Newsletter,* (Ely-Winton Boundary Waters Conservation Alliance), 16 June 1979, 2.

15. Brochure enclosed in *Newsletter* (Ely-Winton Alliance), 16 June 1979. It drew parallels between Alaska and Minnesota, claiming that both states were subject to "land grabs" by the federal government. The Alliance argued against the idea that "ownership of land should not be the right of individuals, but of society as a whole."

16. Frank Salerno, affidavit, 23 July 1979, BWCA Papers, MHS.

17. Louise Leoni, affidavit, 25 July 1979, BWCA Papers, MHS.

18. Steve Jourdain, Sr., affidavit, 21 July 1979, BWCA Papers, MHS. Jourdain's statement was not strictly accurate. In 1979 the superintendent of Quetico Provincial Park made an exception for the Indians living on the north shore of Lac La Croix who were registered guides. They were allowed to use outboard motors on certain lakes in the southwest corner of the park. See Miron Heinselman, affidavit, 23 July 1979, 7.

19. *Minneapolis Tribune,* 18 July 1979.

20. *Newsletter* (Ely-Winton Alliance), 27 July 1979, 4.

21. Ibid.

22. *Minneapolis Tribune,* 22 December 1979.

23. Ibid. Shortly before the state filed the lawsuit, Herbert Johnson, a Republican from Edina, wrote Governor Quie suggesting that he not continue this course of action. He gave several reasons for why the litigation might damage the Republican Party's fortunes in Minnesota politics. Johnson noted that statewide polls showed a majority of citizens approved of greater restrictions on motors in the canoe area. He also noted that Minnesota's media "strongly supported a wilderness character for the BWCA." Johnson argued that the lawsuit would have four negative results. First, it would drive a deeper political wedge between northeastern Minnesota and the rest of the state. Second, it would create public hostility toward the Quie Administration for stirring up the BWCA controversy. Third, it would be used as a campaign issue by DFL candidates to turn Republicans out of state offices. Fourth, the action had little chance of success and thus could be a waste of state money. See "Letter from Herbert C. Johnson to Governor Albert Quie," 3 December 1979, BWCA Papers, MHS.

24. *Duluth News-Tribune,* 19 January 1980.

25. See "Summary of United States District Court Opinion Dismissing the Three

Challenges to the BWCA Act," letter from Charles Dayton and Richard Rapson to intervenors in the case and other interested parties, 7 August 1980, 2, BWCA Papers, MHS.

26. *National Association of Property Owners v. U.S.,* 499 Supp. 1229 (District of Minnesota, Fifth Division, 1980).

27. Ibid., 1234.

28. Ibid., 1249.

29. Ibid.

30. Ibid., 1233.

31. Ibid., 1260–61.

32. Ibid., 1265.

33. *Newsletter* (Ely-Winton Alliance), August 1980, 2.

34. Ibid.

35. Dayton and Rapson, "Summary of U.S. District Court Opinion," 1.

36. 426 U.S. 529 (1976), 16 *ERC* 2206.

37. 16 *ERC* 2206.

38. *St. Paul Sunday Pioneer Press,* 14 March 1982.

39. *Duluth News-Tribune,* 20 March 1979.

40. Ibid., 11 April 1979.

41. Ibid., 17 January 1980.

42. Ibid., 19 January 1980.

43. Ibid.

44. Ibid., 17 February 1980.

45. Ibid., 26 January 1980.

46. Ibid.

47. Mel Blank et al., *A Needs Assessment of Tourism Firms Serving the Boundary Waters Canoe Area Wilderness Vicinity* (St. Paul: Agricultural Extension Service, University of Minnesota, 1980), 1.

48. Ibid.

49. Ibid., 2.

50. Ibid., 29.

51. Ibid., 30.

52. Ibid., 40. Julia Gardner and John Marsh divide outdoor recreationists into those oriented toward consumption and those who prefer activities that conserve the environment. The consumer engages in leisure actions that use more resources, such as operating off-road vehicles and mobile homes. The conserver engages in outdoor activity such as hiking, bird watching, and other actions that have a light impact on the land. See Gardner and Marsh, "Recreation in Consumer and Conserver Societies," *Alternatives* 7 (Summer 1978): 25–29. Frank Brockman and Lawrence Merriam, Jr. distinguish between physical and cultural values in outdoor recreation. The former includes canoeing, hiking, and climbing; the latter includes taking photographs and studying nature. They argue that while the pursuit of cultural values in a wilderness area promotes physical values, the physical effort is a means to attain cultural values, not an end in itself. See Brockman and Merriam, *Recreational Use of Wild Lands,* 2d ed. (New York: McGraw-Hill Book Co., 1973), 17.

53. *Duluth Sunday News-Tribune,* 2 August 1981.

54. U.S. Forest Service, *Plan to Implement the Boundary Waters Canoe Area Wilderness Act* (Duluth, Minn.: Superior National Forest, 1981), 3.

55. Ibid., 5.

56. For a discussion of the ROS concept, see Daniel L. Dustin and Leo H. Mc-

Avoy, "The Decline and Fall of Quality Recreation Opportunities and Environments?" *Environmental Ethics* 4 (Spring 1982): 49–57. The ROS was developed by the U.S. Forest Service in a 1979 report. It was designed to provide recreationists with different environmental settings, depending on their preferences. See Roger N. Clark and George H. Stankey, "The Recreation Opportunity Spectrum: A Framework for Planning, Management, and Research," U.S. Department of Agriculture, Forest Service, Pacific Northwest Forest and Range Experiment Station, General Technical Report, PNW-98, December 1979.

57. U.S. Forest Service, *Plan,* 31.

58. An agency document stated, "While the Forest Service does not regulate use on the water surface, it does control what is transported over portages that are on federal land." USDA-FS-R9-FES-Adm-74-1, 2. The state of Minnesota also promulgated NR 1000, "Use of State Lands and Waters Within the Boundary Waters Canoe Area." These regulations were written to make state policies for managing the area identical to provisions in the Freeman directives of 1965. NR 1000 says, "All waters in streams and lakes within the State that are capable of substantial public use are public waters subject to the control of the State." Ibid., 65.

59. For a study of wilderness overuse impacts, see L. C. Merriam and R. F. Peterson, "Impact of Fifteen Years of Use on Some Campsites in the Boundary Waters Canoe Area," *Minnesota Forestry Research Notes,* (College of Forestry, University of Minn., St. Paul) no. 282 (April 1983).

60. Several sources have confirmed that no specific numbers exist on the effects of the BWCA Wilderness Act of 1978 on Ely's economic situation. The U.S. Forest Service is a potential source of data on the economic effects of the statute, but Toivo Sober stated that the agency had no figures on this complex question (interview with author on 5 August 1983, Duluth, Minn.). In response to an inquiry by the author, the Ely Chamber of Commerce indicated that the economic effects were generally negative, but the chamber was unable to supply specific information (letter dated 20 September 1983 in BWCA files at Department of Political Science/Justice, University of Alaska Fairbanks). Robert Cary, editor of the *Ely Echo,* argued that the law slowed the economy because many clients who had used motors over the years assumed that all engines were banned and stopped coming (interview, 4 August 1983, Ely, Minn.). Woods Davis, an outfitter on Moose Lake, argued that eleven of fifteen resorts along the Fernberg Road east of Ely were forced to close as a result of the law hurting their businesses. He also stated that his outfitting business had lost profitable fishing camp operations on Basswood Lake because of motor bans in P.L. 95-495 (interview with author, 18 January 1983, Indianapolis, Ind.). Another Ely outfitter, Robert Olson, argued that he had lost business as a result of the new statute because now more BWCA visitors outfitted themselves (interview with author, 2 August 1983, Ely, Minn.). Russell Robertson, president of the Ely-Winton Alliance and owner of an automobile parts store, contended that the general volume of business in the community was down; fewer tourists came through the town, and those who did spent less money (interview with author, 1 August 1983, Ely, Minn.). Other area businessmen interviewed expressed similar negative views about the effects of the statute on the town and surrounding area.

61. For a discussion of the "love of place," see Yi-Fu Tuan, *Topophilia: A Study of Environmental Perceptions, Attitudes, and Values* (Englewood Cliffs, N.J.: Prentice-Hall, 1974). David Seamon also analyzes the attachment to a geographical area through a study of William Wordsworth's "Tinturn Abbey," written in 1789. See "Emotional Experience of the Environment," *American Behavioral Scientist* 27 (July–August 1984): 757–70.

CHAPTER 7

1. See Aldo Leopold, *A Sand County Almanac: With Essays on Conservation from Round River* (New York: Ballantine Books, 1970), 270.

2. Garrett Hardin, "The Economics of Wilderness," *Natural History* 78 (June 1969): 24–25. Sigurd Olson relates a story in which he chartered a floatplane to fly him from Ely to Lake Gabemichigami for a short visit. As he ate lake trout by the evening campfire and listened to the loons, Olson reflected that "for the first time in my life I had failed to work for the joy of knowing the wilderness, had not given it a chance to become a part of me." He mused that while the last time he had visited this lake it had taken three days of canoe paddling, "this time it actually seemed that I had not earned the right to enjoy it." Olson noted, however, that flying over the area had given him a view of the canoe area "that I could not have had in any other way, and the beauty was not lost to me." See "Flying In," in *The Singing Wilderness* (New York: Alfred A. Knopf, 1956), 112–16.

3. Arthur Carhart, "Jeeps in the Wilderness," *American Forests* 54 (January 1949): 14–15. Carhart's ideas on motorized travel in wilderness areas are similar to Hardin's tragedy of the commons. He argues that limits must be placed on the use of a resource in public or common ownership. If not, it may be overused and even destroyed, as in the case of a salmon run or a wilderness area. For example, Hardin argues that if limits are not placed on the amount and type of recreational use allowed in Yosemite National Park, the purpose for which people visit the park will be destroyed. See "The Tragedy of the Commons," *Science* 162 (13 December 1968): 1243–48.

4. Ibid.

5. Allan Pospisil, "Ski Tour of a Threatened Wilderness," *Skiing Holiday* 31 (January 1979): 116.

6. See Dorothy H. Anderson, "The Effect of User Experience on Displacement," in *Proceedings of Applied Geography Conferences,* vol. 4, October 22–24, 1981, Tempe, Ariz., ed. J. W. Frazier and B. J. Epstein (Binghamton: Department of Geography, State University of New York, 1981): 272–79.

7. Sid Moody, "Wilderness: A Key to Survival?" 114 *Congressional Record* S11079 (30 April 1968).

8. Sigurd Olson, "What is Wilderness?," *The Living Wilderness* 32 (Spring 1968): 7.

9. See Roderick Nash, "International Concepts of Wilderness Management," in *Wilderness Management* ed. John C. Hendee et al., 48. For a discussion of criteria for wilderness size based on ecological science, see Roger Lewin, "Parks: How Big is Enough?" *Science* 225 (10 August 1984): 611–12.

10. Ibid.

11. For example, see Riley Dunlap, "Paradigmatic Change in Social Science," *American Behavioral Science* 24 (September–October 1980): 13. Dunlap argues, "The social sciences have largely ignored the fact that human societies depend on the biophysical environment for their survival." Dunlap claims this is because these disciplines developed in an era of material abundance, before ecological constraints appeared on the horizon. See also Thomas S. Kuhn, *The Structure of Scientific Revolutions* (Chicago: University of Chicago Press, 1970), 23. Kuhn refers to a paradigm as a model or form of restricted vision in which a group of people think about a set of problems. For example, the plate tectonics model is used by earth scientists to explain geological events such as earthquakes and volcanoes.

12. See William Ophuls, *Ecology and the Politics of Scarcity* (San Francisco: W. H. Freeman and Co., 1977). Ophuls argues that modern civilization confronts a global environmental crisis. He promotes a reorienting of basic attitudes toward the place of humans in the natural scheme of things.

13. John Locke, *Two Treatises of Government,* ed. Peter Laslett, (New York: Cambridge University Press, 1960), 327–44.

14. William R. Catton and Riley E. Dunlap, "A New Ecological Paradigm for Post-Exuberant Sociology," *American Behavioral Scientist* 24 (September–October 1980): 15–47.

15. Ibid., 34.

16. See William R. Catton, *Overshoot: The Ecological Basis of Revolutionary Change* (Urbana: University of Illinois Press, 1980). For a similar perspective, see Mihajlo Mesarovic and Edward Pestel, *Mankind at the Turning Point: The Second Report to the Club of Rome* (New York: E. P. Dutton and Co., 1974). There is considerable debate on the extent to which resource depletion and ecosystem disruption is occurring and the role of science and technology in solving these problems. For a study that challenges the ecological scarcity thesis, see H. S. Cole, et al., *Models of Doom: A Critique of the Limits to Growth* (New York: Universe Books, 1973).

17. Aldo Leopold, "The Land Ethic," in *A Sand County Almanac,* 237–64. For another statement of the new environmental paradigm, see William Devall and George Sessions, *Deep Ecology: Living as if Nature Mattered* (Salt Lake City: Gibbs M. Smith, Inc., 1985). Also see Lester W. Milbrath, *Environmentalists: Vanguard for a New Society* (Albany: State University of New York Press, 1986).

18. In the BWCA case, the issue of acid rain began with a proposal in 1973 by Ontario Hydro to build an eight-hundred-megawatt coal-fired power plant in Atikokan, a small town on the northern border of Quetico Provincial Park. Atikokan, which means "caribou bones" in Ojibwa, was located only forty miles from the BWCA. American environmentalists were concerned that the power station, if built, would damage BWCA watersheds, which had a low tolerance for acid loading. The controversy ended in 1979, when Ontario Hydro officials decided not to follow through on the project, primarily because the projected demand for electricity was not high enough. See John E. Carroll, *Environmental Diplomacy: An Examination and a Prospective of Canadian-U.S. Transboundary Environmental Relations* (Ann Arbor: University of Michigan Press, 1983), 216–23.

19. John C. Hendee and George H. Stankey, "Biocentricity in Wilderness Management," *BioScience* 23 (September 1973): 535–38. In their definition, the biocentric concept is human-centered. Wilderness lands should be allowed to remain intact insofar as they provide benefits for people. This differs from a life-centered view of the idea, which sees wilderness as a value in itself.

20. Richard J. Costley, "An Enduring Resource," *American Forests* 78 (June 1972): 8.

21. Eric Jubler, "Let's Open Up Our Wilderness Areas," *Reader's Digest* 100 (May 1972): 125–28.

SELECTED BIBLIOGRAPHY

Ahlgren, Clifford, and Ahlgren, Isabel. *Lob Trees in the Wilderness*. Minneapolis: University of Minnesota Press, 1984.

Allin, Craig W. *The Politics of Wilderness Preservation*. Westport, Conn.: Greenwood Press, 1982.

Ashby, Eric. *Reconciling Man with the Environment*. Stanford, Calif.: Stanford University Press, 1978.

Baldwin, Donald N. *The Quiet Revolution: Grass Roots of Today's Wilderness Preservation Movement*. Boulder, Colo.: Pruett Publishing Co., 1972.

Bartlett, Robert V. *The Reserve Mining Controversy: Science, Technology, and Environmental Quality*. Bloomington: Indiana University Press, 1980.

Beymer, Robert. *The Boundary Waters Canoe Area*. Volume 2. *The Eastern Region*. Berkeley, Calif.: The Wilderness Press, 1979.

Brooks, Paul. *The Pursuit of Wilderness*. Boston: Houghton Mifflin Co., 1971.

Cahn, Robert. *Footprints on the Planet: A Search for an Environmental Ethic*. New York: Universe Books, 1978.

Caldwell, Lynton K. *Environment: A Challenge to Modern Society*. Garden City, New York: Doubleday & Co., 1970.

Catton, William R., Jr. *Overshoot: The Ecological Basis of Revolutionary Change*. Urbana: University of Illinois Press, 1980.

Cooley, Richard A., and Wandesford-Smith, Geoffrey, eds. *Congress and the Environment*. Seattle: University of Washington Press, 1970.

Devall, Bill, and Sessions, George. *Deep Ecology: Living as if Nature Mattered*. Salt Lake City: Gibbs M. Smith, 1985.

Frome, Michael. *Battle for the Wilderness*. New York: Praeger Publishers, 1974.

Hardin, Garrett, and Baden, John, eds. *Managing the Commons*. San Francisco: W. H. Freeman and Co., 1977.

Hays, Samuel P. *Beauty, Health, and Permanence: Environmental Politics in the United States, 1955–1985*. New York: Cambridge University Press, 1987.

Hendee, John C., Stankey, George H., and Lucas, Robert C. *Wilderness Management*. Washington, D.C.: U.S. Forest Service, Miscellaneous Publication No. 1365, 1978.

Huth, Hans. *Nature and the American*. Berkeley: University of California Press, 1957.

Leopold, Aldo. *A Sand County Almanac: With Essays on Conservation from Round River*. New York: Ballantine Books, 1970.

Mann, Dean E., ed. *Environmental Policy Formation: The Impact of Values, Ideology, and Standards*. Lexington, Mass.: Lexington Books, 1981.

Marshall, Robert. *Alaska Wilderness: Exploring the Central Brooks Range*. 2d ed. Berkeley: University of California Press, 1970.

May, Allan. *Voice in the Wilderness*. Chicago: Nelson-Hall, 1978.

Milbrath, Lester. *Environmentalists: Vanguard for a New Society*. Albany: State University of New York Press, 1985.

Nash, Roderick. *Wilderness and the American Mind*. rev. 3d ed. New Haven, Conn.: Yale University Press, 1983.

Neuhaus, Richard. *In Defense of People: Ecology and the Seduction of Radicalism*. New York: The Macmillan Co., 1977.

Nute, Grace Lee. *The Voyageur's Highway: Minnesota's Border Lake Land*. St. Paul: Minnesota Historical Society Press, 1941.

Olson, Sigurd. *The Singing Wilderness*. New York: Alfred A. Knopf, 1956.

Ophuls, William. *Ecology and the Politics of Scarcity*. San Francisco: W. H. Freeman and Co., 1977.

Robinson, Glenn O. *The Forest Service: A Study in Public Land Management*. Baltimore: The Johns Hopkins University Press, 1975.

Roth, Dennis M. *The Wilderness Movement and the National Forest Service*. College Station, Texas: The Intaglio Press, 1988.

Searle, R. Newell. *Saving Quetico-Superior: A Land Set Apart*. St. Paul: Minnesota Historical Society Press, 1977.

Tribe, Lawrence H., Schelling, Corrine S., and Voss, John. *When Values Conflict: Essays on Environmental Analysis, Discourse, and Decision*. Cambridge, Mass.: Ballinger Press, 1976.

Tucker, William. *Progress and Privilege: America in the Age of Environmentalism*. Garden City, New York: Doubleday & Co., 1982.

INDEX

Agricultural Extension Service, 98–99
Alexander, Joseph, 77
Ambrose, Ben, 100
Anderson, Irvin, 59–60
Anderson, Wendell, 71, 72–73, 75, 83
Andrews, Christopher, 16–17
Arrowhead region, 88, 100–102
Aviation industry, 26. *See also*
  Recreation, motorized use

Backus, E. W., 17
Blatnik, John, 30, 31, 47
Boundary Waters Canoe Area
  (BWCA)
  appropriations, 96–98
  conflicts, 23–24, 27, 34–35, 89–90.
    See also Judicial review;
    Industry; Recreation
  ecology, 10–11, 14–15, 19, 112–15
  economic development, 27, 33–35
  geography, 3, 13–14
  history, 3–6, 15–21. *See also*
    BWCA, legislation
  implementation, 99–100
  industry. *See* Industry
  legislation, 5, 6–7, 26–27, 43, 44–
    45, 47–63, 67–80, 87–96
  management, 23, 32, 35, 36. *See*
    also U.S. Forest Service
  passage, 73–80
  policy, 17
  recreational use. *See* Recreation
  zoning, 32, 40, 49, 67, 100, 140n.54
Boundary Waters Canoe Area
  Wilderness Act of 1978, 4, 8, 43,
    44, 50, 52, 59. *See also* BWCA,

legislation; Appendix 2
Boundary Waters Conservation
  Alliance. *See* Interest Groups,
  Alliance
Boundary Waters Resources
  Committee, 33–35, 37, 41, 50
Boundary Waters Review Committee,
  30
Brown, Carl, 93
Brown, Russell, 63
Buckler, Robert, 53
Burton, Phillip, 55, 58–59, 68, 83. *See*
  also Burton-Vento Bill; House
  Subcommittee on National Parks
  and Insular Affairs
Burton-Vento Bill, 67–69, 73–76
Butz, Earl, 7, 39, 41, 42

Carhart, Arthur, 19, 108
Carter administration, 62, 84
Cary, Robert, 57–58
Catton, William, 112–15
Chelesnik, John, 109
Cherry, Jim, 54
Costley, Richard, 116
Cotgrove, S. F., 63
Cravens, Jay, 36
Crane Lake, 52
Cutler, Rupert, 21

Dayton, Charles, 36, 48, 49, 90, 95.
  See also Dayton-Walls
  compromise
Dayton-Walls compromise, 76–78, 83
Democratic Farmer-Labor Party, 72

Dunlap, Riley, 112–15

Economics. *See* Industry
Ely, town of, 16, 26–27, 33, 44, 52,
    59, 97, 148n.60. *See also* Public
    opinion.
Ely Echo, 56, 57
Environmental values, 7–11, 19, 26,
    30, 51, 83, 105–17. *See also*
    Interest groups, Friends, Sierra
    Club, Wilderness Society

Federal agencies. *See* U.S. Department
    of Agriculture
Forest Reserves Act, 16
Fraser, Donald, 6, 44, 51–52, 56, 58,
    72
Freeman, Orville, 30–33, 35, 54
Friends of the Boundary Waters
    Wilderness. *See* Interest groups,
    Friends

Grand Marais, town of, 38, 44, 52, 59
Green, Janet, 61
Greene, Harold, 90

Hall, Alvin, 69
Hardin, Garrett, 107
Heinselman, Miron, 41, 49, 51, 56
Herbst, Robert, 50
House Committee on Interior and
    Insular Affairs, 73
House Subcommittee on National
    Parks and Insular Affairs, 55, 83
Human Exemptionalist Paradigm,
    112–15
Humphrey, Hubert, 20, 26–27, 28, 29,
    30–33, 44, 82
Humphrey, Muriel, 75

Industry
    aviation, 26
    conflicts, 27–29, 49, 55, 59, 62, 63–
        65, 74–75
    mining, 21–22, 23, 28, 40

timber, 16, 17, 19, 22, 23, 26–27,
    28, 30, 40, 43, 48, 62
tourist, 26, 28, 90, 97–99
International Joint Commission, 17–
    18
International Root-Bryce Treaty, 17
Interest groups
    Alliance, 5, 6, 52–53, 56, 61, 62,
        64, 68, 69–72, 74, 75–78, 80–
        82, 86, 87, 89, 91–93, 94, 102,
        110
    Audubon Society, 40, 61
    Boating Industry associations, 60
    Friends, 5, 6, 41, 49, 51–52, 53, 62,
        64, 68, 70, 73–74, 75–78, 80–
        82, 83–84, 88, 95, 102, 110
    Izaak Walton League, 21, 25, 31,
        34, 40, 49, 57, 68, 88
    Minnesota Federation of Ski
        Touring Clubs, 36, 41
    National Association of Property
        Owners, 87, 89
    Sierra Club, 36, 56, 90
    Timber Producers Association, 31
    Wilderness Society, 10, 20, 41, 68,
        75

Jardine, William, 25
Johnson, Douglas, 72
Johnson, Lenore, 78
Jourdain, Steve, 90
Jubler, Eric, 116–117
Judicial review, 21–22, 43, 44–45,
    92–96
    decisions, 27–28, 41–43, 89–96
    rulings, 44–45, 92–94

Kaufman, Matthew, 60
Kleppe v. New Mexico, 95
Knopp, Timothy, 61–62

Lac La Croix Indian Reserve, 90
Leoni, Louise, 89–90
Leopold, Aldo, 107
Locke, John, 111
Lord, Miles, 22, 43, 92–94